To Meg and Les, I hope you enjoy the book — and Calera 'Pinot Noirs'! Josh Jensen 11/23/93

THE
HEARTBREAK GRAPE

A CALIFORNIA WINEMAKER'S SEARCH FOR THE PERFECT PINOT NOIR

by

Marq De Villiers

HarperCollinsWest
A Division of HarperCollinsPublishers

HarperCollinsWest and the author, in association with the Rainforest Action Network, will facilitate the planting of two trees for every one tree used in the manufacture of this book.

FIRST EDITION

Library of Congress Cataloging-in-Publication Data

De Villiers, Marq.
The heartbreak grape : a California winemaker's search for the perfect pinot noir / Marq de Villiers. — 1st ed.
p. cm.

ISBN 0-06-258523-1

1. Pinot noir (Wine)—California.
2. Calera Wine Company.
3. Wine and wine making—California. I. Title.

TP557.D43 1994   93-25625   641.2′223—dc20   CIP

94 95 96 97 98 ❖ RRD 10 9 8 7 6 5 4 3 2 1

This edition is printed on acid-free paper that meets the American National Standards Institute Z39.48 Standard.

Contents

XVI

*In which the wines are priced,
distributors are found, and the wines are
taken out into the world for their
final date with the consumer*

page 175

A marvelous searching wine, and it perfumes the blood ere
one can say, 'what's this?'

Tasting note, W. Shakespeare

I

*In which a bottle of wine is
consumed, and some inquiries
into the grand conceit of its
origins are undertaken*

Outside, the sun was slanting down over the golden California hills, warm and still on this October afternoon, but inside the great vaulted cellar of the Calera Wine Company the air was cool, damp, heady, vinous. Josh Jensen, the owner, strategist and propagandist-in-chief of Calera, eased a silicone bung from one of the racked barrels and it came away with a soft, sighing hiss, a faint carbonic prickle adding itself to the damp-oak and washed-earth and crushed-fruit smells of the winery. I closed my eyes and inhaled deeply and the aroma went directly, as aromas do, to the vaults in the brain where nostalgic memories are stored, and I remembered the great limewashed cellars of the Cape, where as a child I had played among oaken casks as big as houses, cool and serene despite the burning African sun. Memories welled up—farm workers in big Wellington boots, unhurried and competent; lowing cattle, fresh hay, crushed grapes sticky with sugar, racks of bottles on dusty shelves, a cat sleeping in the entranceway, curled in the shade, a paw over its eyes. The farmer would bring visitors into the cellar, big buyers from the city, and they'd step over the cat and be seduced by the smells and the farmer would draw off a little wine to taste, and after a while they'd leave and the farmer would be smiling. In my memory he always seemed to be smiling.

I pulled my attention back to the cellar. Josh Jensen laid the bung on the barrel, alongside a small cloth and a plastic bucket. "These are made of some kind of silicone compound. We don't use wood bungs any more. Who says we're against technology at our winery!"

Whoever it was, it hadn't been me. But this was a small phrase in a longer dialogue about winemaking, and I knew we'd come back to it. I did know that the old wooden bungs were always a problem for wine-makers; after a while the moisture would wick up along the grain and the bung had to be wiped clean with sulfur dioxide or the wine would spoil. And if there was still fermentation going on in the barrel, the bungs could explode outwards; many a winemaker, incautiously lean-ing over the barrel, was banged on the head. Occasionally, someone

lost an eye. The new soft silicone stoppers were easy to get out and impervious to moisture.

There were four wineglasses on an upturned barrel that served as a table. Jensen picked up his "thief," a slender glass pipette about a foot long that looked rather like a turkey baster, and slipped it into the bunghole. He drew out enough wine to fill the glasses about a third. Sara Steiner, Calera's winemaker, and Diana Vita, the winery manager, picked up a glass each and Josh another. The last was for me. I dipped my nose into the new wine. There was a strong fruitiness to the aroma and a complex of other odors too elusive to detect, flowery, like crushed raspberries on a summer's day. I took a sip. It was tannic and made my mouth pucker. Again, those elusive scents—there was an underlying silkiness that came from the oak, a faint hint of fresh farm butter.

I stared at the wine, then into it, holding it up to the light. It glowed, a brilliant polished ruby. I moved back a few paces until the glass was framed in the doorway; beyond it I could see the high hills of the Gavilan range, wave after wave of silky golden brown folds in the landscape, dotted here and there with oak trees, fold after fold of gold, smooth and erotic, like the skin of an inner thigh. In the far distance the air was smoky, a blue haze melting into the golden grass. I could hear a cow mooing in the distance, a melancholy sound.

With difficulty, I turned away from the view. Josh Jensen was sniffing and swirling his glass. He peered at the label on the barrel. "Hmmm," he said. "Early picking from the Mills vineyard. New oak. Still very closed, but coming along nicely."

Steiner made notes. "Nice fruit," she said.

"Yes," Jensen said. "The late pickings will be less fruity than this, more opulent, much much more complex. Put them together and you'll have something wonderful here."

This last was directed at me, in an instructional and not propagandistic way—there's some reason to believe that all of Josh Jensen's wines are wonderful in their way. I was here because I'd become interested in the process of winemaking, and Jensen at his Calera winery was supposed to be making some of the best and most

Burgundian pinot noir in America (a place where, until recently, you were not supposed to be able to make great wines from the pinot noir grape). His notion of early, middle and late pickings in the vineyard was one small part of his technique. Although when it came right down to it, I discovered later, I was really still missing the point. What he was telling me was, be respectful of the fruit—give it a gallant bow as it passes through from vintage to bottle and don't get in its way more than you absolutely have to. I was somewhat reminded of a snatch of dialogue from a Dick Francis murder mystery called *Proof*, in which the hero is a wine merchant. The investigating cop, as stolid as most fictional cops, watches as the hero sells a bottle to a customer and dispenses advice along with it:

> "'You sell knowledge, don't you, as much as wine?'
> 'Yeah. And pleasure. And human contact.'
> 'Is there anything you can't drink wine with?'
> 'As far as I'm concerned ... grapefruit.' He made a face. 'And that's from one,' I said, 'who drinks wine with baked beans ... who practically scrubs his teeth with it.'
> 'You really love it?'
> I nodded. 'Nature's magical accident.'
> 'What?'
> 'That the fungus on the grape turns the sugar in grape juice to alcohol. That the result is delicious.'
> 'For heaven's sake ...'
> 'No one could have invented it,' I said. 'It's just there. A gift to the planet.'"

A gift of nature!

Well, and so is the potato, I suppose. But no matter how crisp the *frite*, how silky the mash (no matter that the potato can be the color of gold or a ghastly industrial blue), potato eaters and growers are not united into a community of interest in the way wine people are—potato shops are not places where culture and agriculture meet (there's no art, only sound craft, to growing them); individual potato fields do not change hands at astronomical prices; there are no specialized potato shops (1991 Yukon Golds, a great year!) or potato tastings; no one collects vintage potatoes or keeps cellar books detailing their virtues. The potato is a humble thing and so, in its way, is the vine.

I picked up my glass and carried it back to the doorway. It now contained wine from a different barrel, and it too was brilliantly clear, limpid. I took a sip, pulling it through my teeth the way winetasters do. The vine, I thought, might be humble, but wine is not humble at all. Wine has almost infinite variety and complexity, an ability at once to surprise and overwhelm the most sophisticated palate and to give simple pleasure to millions of people. Wine is international, virtually universal, with a history almost as old as man, with its own litany and lore, with its own poetics of sensation, with its own rituals (the formal tastings) and craft (more care is taken in making wine barrels than in making many complex industrial artifacts). Winemaking can be a complicated industrial process or a simple thing to do in a crock at home, but the makers of great wine are magnificently obsessed, cease-lessly self-questioning, constantly attempting to move their product towards some elusive and ineffable ideal.

I looked out again at the California hills and thought of the community that wine represents. It stretches from Calera across the Atlantic to the stony slopes of the Côte d'Or, in Burgundy, the center of the pinot noir universe, and from there to the drawing rooms of Knightsbridge, the salons of Park Avenue and the manor houses of the Hunter Valley.

Down the road from Calera, over the beautiful desolation of the Gavilan Mountains, is the wine estate called Chalone; its proprietors not only make superior pinot noir but their lives have intersected with Jensen's in interesting ways.

Inland, amid the almond groves of the Central Valley, are the mas-sive tank farms of the Gallos, who have come the closest of anyone in the winemaking business to succeeding at that very American task, the reduction of art to a diligent industrialism, to chemistry and mar-keting. And yet the Gallos, marketers par excellence (one out of every three bottles sold in America is a Gallo wine), also feel the nee-dle-pricks that tell them some things are beyond *process*, and are pouring money and resources into *quality*. It's like watching someone trying to pour the Pacific Ocean through a funnel into a five-gallon jug, like watching an ocean liner docking in a yacht harbor—if they bring it off, their artistry will be universally admired. If not, the purists will be confirmed in their definitions of folly.

Further north, in a pretty little town, is the school of viticulture and enology of the University of California at Davis, usually shortened to just "Davis" as in, "I don't want to be a Davis-basher, but ..." These are the folks who brought you that blue potato and the square tomato, for whom the chemistry of wine is their prime mandate. Davis is the repository of enological orthodoxy, the proselytizer of viticultural hygiene, the Keeper of the Recipe, the people who made possible the Gallos, the people who rescued the American wine industry after Prohibition from oblivion (and also from the fruit fly, the vinegar bacterium, sundry diseases and pests), the people who have encouraged the production of good clean wines, well made, polished, safe, hygienic, characterless. How many times have I heard winemakers say of their new Davis recruits—people skilled at the chemistry of winemaking—that they first had to unlearn their Davis lessons before they could fully grasp, emotionally as well as technically, the idea of great wine. Or, at the least, they had to learn through mistakes to understand something profound about wine, which is that nature is older than they are and has more tricks up her provocative sleeve than will ever be discovered in the refractometers and centrifuges of the laboratory. They had to learn that what they did was not manufacturing, as they had been taught, but midwifery; they had to understand, as Colette wrote, that "wine makes the true savor of the earth intelligible to man." Nikos Kazantzakis, whose lush romanticism was once cherished in fevered teenaged diaries (before the days of Guns 'n' Roses), called the drinking of wine "communion with the blood of the earth itself," a typically overwrought notion, but you get what he means.

Further away, up the North Coast and a million miles in sensibility from the Gallos, are the agricultural communities of Napa and Sonoma, where farmers have become successful through skill and superior marketing (there are people humble and smug in both places; also people who have made for themselves an exceptionally gracious lifestyle—and people who are rapidly going broke).

Considerably north of Napa, in the Willamette valley of Oregon, are farmers toiling on the edge of climatic plausibility, as do the growers of the Côte d'Or in their venerable postage-stamp plots with their resonant names—the Domaine de la Romanée-Conti, La Tâche, les Echézeaux, Clos de Vougeot.

The wine community stretches to the great merchants of New York and London, to the wholesalers, shippers, importers and distributors, to the fogs of Carneros in California, to the silky folds in the mountains around Fransch Hoek in South Africa, to the fertile valleys of the central Chilean plains, to the stony fields of La Mancha and the gentle sheep meadows of New Zealand. And to the most surprising pastures—England, the Black Sea coast of Russia, even to that most unlikely of all *domaines*, Long Island. It reaches also from the *haut snob* wine shops of London through the idiosyncratic stores of New York to the massive warehouses of California ("Liquors and Ammo!" the signs say) and down into the neighborhood *boîtes* of Paris, where they sell the acidic plonk of the Midi *en plastique*. And, finally, it reaches the millions of tables where the corks are pulled and the food is served and pleasure is given and taken.

In the Calera cellar, there were twelve barrels of the 1991 Early Mills vineyard pinot noir and eight of the Late. The vineyard crews had only done two pickings that year; 1991, the fifth year of the drought, was a year of very small yields. We moved on down the rows of neatly stacked barrels, Josh Jensen using the thief at each one to draw out enough to fill our four glasses. We swirled, sipped, spat into the concrete runnels along the floor, Jensen carefully pouring the unused and untasted wine back into the barrels to top them up. Each barrel had a paper docket label stapled to the oak and a stencil denoting its originating cooperage and its year. The dockets would contain scribbles, in various hands and in various colored inks, some of them cryptic to the point of inscrutability—what did "1 K2 14/Y" mean? Other notations were more straightforward:

10/15/91
MILLS EARLY
1/11 finished m-l
1/22 90 ppm SO_2
2/7 30 ppm SO_2.

Which simply meant the wine had been put into barrel on October 15, had finished its secondary, or malolactic, fermentation by January 11 and was twice stabilized by small doses of the antioxidant sodium dioxide, first on January 22 and then again on February 7.

The barrel also bore the notation that it had been made in France by the *tonnellerie*—cooperage—called François Frères, of St. Romain on the Côte d'Or in France, and a large "1-4"—it had been made in April 1991.

I would discover more on all these matters later.

Clear differences emerged as we moved along the rows. The Mills Early was a touch more astringent, the Mills Late much softer. Steiner, a rather shy woman with a wonderful smile, was making notes on a small clipboard. She'd write down her own observations and some of the comments of the others. "Green tannin," "very consistent," "rich oaky," "a little flat," "quite closed." Is the Early a little "lean," the Late a little "top-heavy"? That's good—each picking contributes its character to the amalgam of the finished wine.

The oak taste of the wine from new barrels, about a third of the batch, was clearly evident—it contributed much of the silky, buttery quality. Josh could also tell the difference between the barrels of François Frères and his other suppliers, whose barrels, he said, made the wine taste a hint too "resiny."

I asked him why that was so.

"I don't know," he said, somewhat disarmingly. "It's just that pinot noir and François Frères are friends. Or at least, my wines and François Frères are friends."

These samplings will continue every couple of weeks throughout the fifteen months the wine is in barrel. Comparisons are made, progress noted. If something is going wrong in a barrel—as it occasionally does—they'll know it soon enough and either correct it, if it's correctable, or eliminate it from the batches marked for later amalgamation.

Afterwards, the de-selected batches will either be sold at a few pennies a gallon to a distillery, marked for blending into a lesser wine, or poured away, the precious juice soaking into the parched California earth.

That morning, one of the barrels was marked to be kept separate from the others, to be kept away from the composite finished wines. The vines from which the juice came were grown with a new experimental trellis system and Jensen wanted to know if he could detect a difference in the finished wine.

Later, Steiner would do sample composites from the various Mills vineyard batches and run analyses in her lab. I asked her what she was looking for.

"Just making sure everything is right," she said, "but it's also for me. I've only been here a short time, since August. This is my first Calera vintage. I want to use these tests to get to know the personalities of the different vineyard parcels and the characters of the wines they make."

Personalities? Characters? And the other words so casually used around serious winemakers — Forwardness? Reserve? Shyness? Approachability? Seductiveness? Eagerness? What is this, a debutantes' ball? This anthropomorphizing would turn the stomachs of the professors at Davis, where they prefer to believe that flavor can be captured through rigorous analysis of long-chain polymers and that winemaking is essentially applied chemistry. But then in Jensen's view, theirs is a barren exercise. He believes they haven't learned the first thing about the craft — that to make good wine is a skill but to make great wine is an art; that wine can be cherished into excellence as well as manufactured; that winemaking is an emotional as well as an industrial task; that the search for perfectibility is a legitimate and a grand obsession. He thinks the professors are boring. They think he takes unnecessary risks for invisible returns.

It's one of the great things about wine, though. Everyone is right.

I was in the Calera cellars because of a particular bottle of wine.

After a while I'd come to think of it, somewhat portentously, as The Bottle, though there was nothing portentous about the place its cork was pulled, a comfortable suburban dining room in the comfortable middle-class enclave of Mount Vernon, New York, and certainly nothing pretentious about the host who pulled its cork or the guests who drank the proffered wine.

It was December and there was a log fire crackling in the hearth. The room was painted in honey yellow; there were piles of books everywhere (the host had been a publisher) and there was a striking painting of the hostess on the wall, her beautiful Renaissance profile in graceful outline. The host took the bottle from his "cellar," a small cupboard underneath the stereo, and pulled the cork without comment, pouring a little of the wine into glasses on the table. I remember that something struck me about its clarity, a brilliant red, like rubies under fire, and though my memory is probably colored by the warmth of the setting, I know I felt there was something ... unusual ... about it.

I looked at the label. It was simple, typographically elegant in an old-fashioned way, with very few words. Not as prolix as many California wine labels, no drawings by eminent artists, no depictions of swooping eagles, hawks, prancing stags or the other wildlife so beloved of logo designers. There was a stylized drawing at the top of the label, in a small panel; it looked rather like the entrance to a fort of some kind. Underneath, in black Caslon typeface, were the words "Calera Jensen Mount Harlan Pinot Noir" and underneath the vintage year, 1987, in the same burgundy color as the drawing. Underneath that it said, in much smaller letters, "Grown, produced and bottled by Calera Wine Company, Hollister, California." And still smaller, in italic script, "Table Wine."

So Calera was the producer. What did "Jensen" mean? Why was it in the largest type on the label? And where was Mount Harlan?

I turned the bottle around to read the explanatory label on the back. This was more helpful. It consisted of a map of the Calera vineyards, which looked like small crosshatched patches on the white background, of varying size and orientation, four drawn in the same burgundy color as the front label and two in green. A wiggly black line labeled Indian Creek ran through the north part of the map, a line that I much later discovered had been and still was a source of bitterness and heartbreak at the winery. A small arrow pointing west said "Pacific Ocean 23 mi," and another arrow denoted north. Each crosshatched patch was identified: "Selleck vineyard, 5 acres" (north of Indian Creek); "Reed vineyard, 5 acres;" "Jensen vineyard, 14 acres;" "Mills vineyard, 12 acres." And the two green patches: "Chardonnay vineyard, 6 acres," "Viognier vineyard, 2 acres."

Underneath all this was a small paragraph: "These vineyards are planted on rare, limestone soil in the Gavilan Mountains of San Benito County. They are located 90 miles south of San Francisco, at 2,200 feet elevation. The Selleck, Reed and Jensen were planted in 1975. The Mills, Chardonnay and Viognier were planted in 1984."

The Mount Harlan of the front label was not shown, though it presumably was one of the Gavilan Mountains of San Benito County. Chardonnay was familiar enough, and viognier I knew as a seldom-seen grape variety, but what (or who) were Selleck, Reed, Jensen and Mills?

I took a sip, but my attention was drawn away from the wine by the person to my left, who was expounding on the legacy of Boris Yeltsin, and another conversation to my right, as the host described the arrival of a first grandchild. It wasn't until much later, after a second slice of beef *en croûte* had disappeared and the host poured the last of the Calera Jensen, that I turned back to the wine. This time I paid more attention, dipping my nose into the glass and inhaling slowly, then taking a small sip. It was rich and complex, with a maddening hint of chocolate and violets. I groped for descriptives, as wine people do, without much luck.

"Very nice, isn't it?" said the man to my left, before moving on from Yeltsin to the problems of advertising in a society of high demand and scarce goods. He meant the wine, not the Russian economy.

Nice, yes. It was certainly that.

I wanted to ask the host how much it cost, and where he got it, and where it came from, and how he'd discovered it, but there's nothing more boring at a dinner party than a quiz master and I resisted. Still, I resolved to find out answers to these questions and more. How had the bottle got here? What made the host choose it? What forces of marketing, advertising, retailing put it in his hands? What distribution chain made it possible? What pricing strategy? Did the winemaker make any money from it, or did the middlemen take more than their share? Had the wine writers, those arbiters of vinous fashion, had their say? Had the wine won tastings? The wine was superb—how was it made, in some high-tech factory operation, by some imported Burgundian *maître de chai*, or by some inspired amateur, a refugee from the dental schools of California? How was the finished wine shaped by the vinification methods chosen? Who was the winemaker and what did he think of his art? What was the winery like? What was Mount Harlan like? What did the label mean by "rare, limestone soil?" What did that have to do with anything? How long had the winemaker been making wine? The label said the Jensen vineyard had been planted in 1975—how long does a vine need to mature to produce grapes that make wine like this? What is the climate like at the vineyards and how does it affect the wine? Why pinot noir in the first place? I knew that farmers in California had long referred to it as the "heartbreak grape" because of its fickle nature and its tendency to veer wildly from thin plonk to superb *vins de garde*. Why did this winemaker, whoever he was, have the presumption to believe he could make wine of this quality? Where did he get the vines in the first place? Who planted them? Who cared for them and how? How were they watered, up there in the mountains?

And, most fundamentally, at what point did this winemaker first conceive of making this wine? Could I identify that moment, and trace the wine through its long journey from conception to this moment here, the wine being poured into a glass at a small dinner party in Mount Vernon, New York?

The rest of the meal passed without further comment on the wine. The guests were not wine snobs, and they were content with good food and something good to drink.

It struck me that the winemaker would, in all probability, be content with that as well. If it was true that making fine wine is an art, the purpose of that art is to bring pleasure, and the unknown (to me) maker of Calera Jensen had certainly achieved that.

I resolved to find out. I would go and ask him.

II

In which an ugly winery is found in
a beautiful if unstable place, and
the people are encountered who sent
our bottle into the world

We met for lunch in a San Francisco restaurant called Roti, which is in the Hotel Griffon on the waterfront near the Bay Bridge. The restaurant was a current favorite of the city's foodies and Josh Jensen, having canceled our breakfast meeting, had promised to make a reservation for lunch. He forgot, but showed up twenty minutes later looking somewhat frazzled and we settled down over a bottle of "not bad" chardonnay (not his own). He was in town for a weekend visit with his three kids (Silvie, sixteen, Duggan, thirteen, and Chloe, six), who live most of the time in the city with his ex-wife, Jeanne.

I had spent the morning reading my clipping file. Josh (Jonathan) Jensen was much admired in the wine press. I had seen his wines judged "sublime" by Robert Parker, the critic of the moment, whose prose can be as purple as the cheap wines of the Midi but whose trenchant judgments can make or break a wine, a vintage or a winery. (It was Parker who had virtually invented the pinot noirs of Oregon.) I had seen Jensen's picture in *The Wine Spectator*, hobnobbing with visiting Burgundian eminences. I had read about his winery in Oz Clarke's splendid book, *The New Classic Wines*. I had read reviews of his wines in *Vanity Fair* and *New York* magazine and the London *Sunday Telegraph*, among others. I had read about him in the pages of *Toronto Life*, in the words of that graceful writer James Chatto. The only thing all these writers agreed on was that he made burgundy-style wines, red and white, approaching and sometimes surpassing the great wines of Burgundy itself. Buried in all the prose about the wines were a few words about the man himself. Clarke called him "laid back and fired up at the same time, and slightly careworn." *Wine Magazine* called him "weather-beaten." *The Houston Post* called him "feisty and confident ... a complicated man." The Swiss publication *Divo* called him the "intellectual outsider of the wine business."

Across the table, I could see what they all meant. He has a long Scandinavian face, somewhat mournful in repose. It reminded me of a horse, though I mean this well: the horse is the most elegant of creatures, with its long bones and expressive lips and slyly intelligent eyes. Jensen's is the face of a man who is outdoors much of the time; and since he's almost fifty, the squint-lines are settling in for good. The body is long and rangy, like one of those Nordic skiers you always see crossing the fifty-kilometer finish line at the Olympics minutes ahead of anyone else. Big hands, big bones, big opinions—on American politics (he's a libertarian), on the "eco-terrorists" of California, on his own and other wines, on almost anything he has an articulated, clearly thought-out position. After the chardonnay we ordered a bottle of his own Mills single-vineyard pinot noir—he always eats in restaurants that serve his own wines except when he indulges his passion for sushi, when he usually takes a bottle of his own along. I watched as he began to systematically demolish a spit-roasted chicken, done rare. In a while the chef, Manny Goodman, came out to ingratiate himself. After a little mutual stroking ("I've always admired your wines..." "There were so many good things on the menu I had trouble making up my mind..."), Goodman retired to his stoves and Jensen gave a wry smile. "I'm as much a marketer as a winemaker these days," he said. "Very much part of the business."

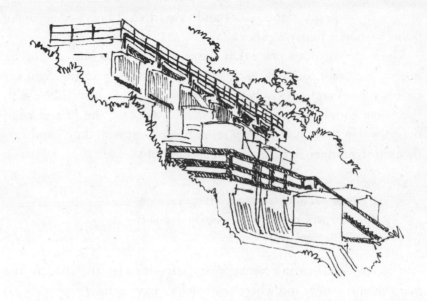

Almost everyone who'd written about the Calera wine operation described it as being located in the "remote Gavilan Mountains," as if they had somehow found themselves in exurban Ulan Bator. For example, the *Companion Wine Review*, in its Spring 1991 issue, referred to "Josh Jensen's bandit hideaway in the Gavilan Mountains, kind of near Chalone Vineyards if you happen to have a Bell Ranger." In truth, Calera is not that remote in geographical terms, being only an hour or so inland from Monterey and not very far from the two main Los Angeles–San Francisco freeways. But in sensibility and feeling it is remote—and remote indeed from the verdant hillsides of Napa or Sonoma, a hundred and fifty miles to the north.

Jensen described his unusual operation in a Spring 1990 mailer to his regular customers because, as he wrote (laying the irony on pretty thick), "Hardly anyone actually visits the winery. Already this year we've had two visitors, and it's only March. We may get two or three more before next winter's snow arrives and cuts us off from the outside world once again. Of course, the two visitors who did find us ran quite a few risks getting here: flat tires courtesy of the puncture weeds, attacks by killer bees, and then there are always those pesky rattlesnakes and crazed wild boar—they make better sausages than neighbors."

The winery is not a place that clasps visitors to its bosom. There's no entrance sign to speak of, just a breakneck turn to the right off Cienega Road and a scratched and battered galvanized mailbox with the name Calera barely visible. A few yards up the gravel road there's a sign that says "Winery tours by appointment only," and further along, another sign, in pure Jensenese, that says,

"Stop! Go Back!
Landmines and rattlesnakes ahead!
Authorized personalities only beyond this point!
Calera Wine Company."

The road to Jensen's house bears left—it's also the road to the maintenance sheds, and where the trucks carrying the grapes will go when they deliver them to the hoppers. To the right, down a sharp incline, is the road to the winery office.

The vineyards are several miles down the road and a million miles away in feeling. If the winery is remote, the vineyards might as well be the Gobi desert. Turn right off Cienega Road onto Limekiln Road and a mile or two in there's a rambling brown house that belongs to Calera's vineyard manager, Jim Ryan. From there, a small dirt road goes up a steep slope. The road winds sharply up the mountain. There are no guard rails and a precipitous, nerve-wracking drop to the right. Near the top is a relatively flat plateau and a locked gate. Past a few cattle pastures, another gate. Beyond that is the Calera reservoir, the subject of almost as many stories as the winery (Jensen feels he's the victim of a vendetta waged by the ecology bureaucrats, a secretive mining company he suspects wants his hilltop and sundry other parties), and the first of his vineyards, six acres of chardonnay.

The soil on the roads and in the vineyards is reddish-white, almost chalky in texture. There are deer everywhere, unsurprised and audacious. In the woods are wild boar. There are rattlesnakes, skunks and gophers, rabbits and birds, and tarantulas on the roads. I stepped gingerly past one, which paused to look me over before scuttling—arrogantly I thought—into the bushes. The limestone kiln pictured on Calera's labels ("Calera" is Spanish for lime kiln) is still there, way up in the mountains, and even higher, much higher than the vineyards, are the ruins of a rock-crushing plant.

On the right are fifteen rows of chardonnay. Further up the canyon are the viognier plantings. Up beyond these are two shallow wells and two more reservoirs, empty and with great runnels punched through them by bulldozers, and more vineyards. At the top a crew is brushing acreage where, money willing, more vines will eventually be planted. To the right of the access road are the named pinot noir plantings, the twelve-acre Mills, the fourteen-acre Jensen, the five-acre Reed and the five-acre Selleck, all of them on steep slopes at crazy angles to the road, facing every which way—the various Mount Harlan vineyards swing almost completely around the cone-shaped mountain top. The Mills, chardonnay and viognier vineyards were planted in 1984. The Selleck, Reed and Jensen were planted in 1975, except for five hundred plants in the Jensen, which were set a year earlier as an experiment.

The wineries of South Africa where I grew up were always—*always*—beautiful as well as functional, and I came to think of beauty as part of the trade, as an integral part of the business. How could it be otherwise? These wineries were set in the rock-ribbed blue mountains of the Cape, in the green and verdant folds in those mountains, and the buildings in which they were housed were the gracious manors in the style called Cape Dutch—low, elegant, thatch-roofed, their limewashed walls thick and cool. Even the cellar buildings at Groot Constantia outside Cape Town were grand enough to pass as a gracious château elsewhere; the Great House at Boschendal in the Drakenstein Mountains, where my family began its South African sojourn, is now a national monument and beautiful beyond compare. The wineries I had visited in France were always at least grand, if occasionally ugly and assertive in that peculiarly French bourgeois manner. And only the day before I'd spent an idyllic couple of hours in Sonoma at the Iron Horse winery, whose hundred-year-old house, meticulously kept and lovingly filled with antiques and objets d'art, is nestled in a stand of ancient sycamores and cedars.

But Calera was not originally built as a manor house or a gentleman's residence, or as a refuge from the city for a wealthy lawyer. It was built as a rock-crushing plant, part of a failed attempt to grind up Mount Harlan into cement, gravel and granite blocks. It's functional, efficient and—not to put too fine a point on it—ugly.

Still, as Oz Clarke put it, "The buildings may be ugly—what rock-crushing plant isn't?—but Calera's owner saw behind the daunting tangle of old weather-stained concrete and rampant weeds something all quality winemakers would love to possess—an entirely gravity-fed winery. At the top of the eight levels he could bring in his boxes of grapes. At the bottom level he could store his bottles to sell. In between, each movement of grape or wine could be by the gentlest of forces—that of gravity."

For Jensen the advantage of a gravity-flow winery is that it eliminates mechanical pumping and handling, and his obsession (or one of his many obsessions) is with minimal handling of the wine during production.

Of course here, in this particular part of California, gravity has another and possibly more sinister meaning. In Hollister, the nearest town, residents had long ago become used to watching parts of their houses drifting slowly away, or tilting, or, indeed, seeing their neighbors' houses slowly getting closer. Cienega Road is plumb in the middle of what the U.S. Geological Survey calls the Central Creeping Zone of the San Andreas Fault. In fact, Cienega Road *is* the San Andreas Fault, which in geological terms is nothing more than a shifting subterranean rubble pile ground between two massive continental plates. Should the Really Big One ever occur, the Calera winery, which is on the very lip of the Pacific Plate, will slide past its neighbors on the other side of Cienega Road, who are firmly anchored to the North American Plate, and disappear into the newly created abyss.

I asked Jensen if the thought ever bothered him, but he gave me that puzzled shrug that all Californians affect when asked the question.

The winery consists of eight levels of retaining concrete walls cascading vertically down the hillside. When the rock-crushing plant was converted to a winery, the engineers insisted on setting reinforcing concrete grade beams in a continuous band from top to bottom, at each level penetrating the earth to thirty or thirty-five feet. At the same time they slung steel I-beams between the verticals. Still, in the '89 earthquake, a three-ton wine press "twirled like a spinning top" on the upper level of the winery. "However, we didn't lose a drop, not a bottle or a barrel." In fact, Calera helped press grapes for another winery, that of David Bruce, which was badly damaged in the quake.

The top level is a roadway leading to the maintenance sheds several hundred yards further up the hillside. The next level down is paved in asphalt to serve as a track for the forklift to carry grapes from the delivery trucks. The grapes arrive from the vineyards in half-ton food-grade plastic bins on a flatbed trailer and the forklift dumps them into hoppers. They fall into one of the eleven stainless-steel fermentation tanks a level below. These are massive things, eight or ten feet tall and wide enough to comfortably contain your average five-piece bathroom. They're all round but one, the largest, which is square and was made to fit exactly between two of the concrete grade beams. Below these tanks are Calera's two presses, covered with bright blue tarps when they're not in use. These are state-of-the-art, exceptionally expensive German stainless-steel presses of twenty-two-hundred-liter and four-thousand-liter capacity. "For a small operation we have very fancy presses," Jensen acknowledges. From the presses the wine drops down another level through flexible food-grade plastic hoses into two large white stainless-steel tanks, forty-five-hundred-gallon and six-thousand-gallon capacity. These have been sprayed on the outside with a white insulation coating and are used only for short-term storage and "settling." From there the wine drops another level to the cellars, where it's stored in barrel. After fifteen months in barrel for the pinot noirs it's drawn off, again by gravity feed, into fining tanks and thence to the bottling line on the warehouse level.

The two upper levels, the fermenting tanks, presses and holding tanks, remain unroofed, exposed to the elements, tarps their only protection. A roof is planned—"as soon as we can afford the hundred thousand dollars it would cost." Only the lowest three levels are covered, with a thirteen-thousand-square-foot galvanized-metal roof. The widest portion is the lowest, the warehouse level. Thence, as Jensen put it in his mailer, "we ship our rare and precious products to a thirsty world."

A small corner of all this, squeezed between two of the grade beams, has been earmarked for an office. For the past ten years the "office" has been a construction trailer on blocks in front of the winery itself. Inside the trailer are two rooms and a large closet. One room is the winemaker's "lab"—here in quotes because it's so laughable. The other room is for the office help and winery management, as well as a dusty photocopy machine, several newish computers and a coffee maker. The winery staff acknowledges that "it would be nice" to have better quarters. Still, it's true they can stare out the windows of their gloomy brown construction trailer at the marvelous hills of California, which must be some compensation.

Another corner of the plant has been earmarked for a tasting and hospitality room, but there's no sign it will ever be built—it'll have to wait until Calera's multiple water problems have been solved, until a new bottling line has been set in place and the two upper levels have been roofed. If one of the star chefs of San Francisco comes to visit (which they sometimes do), bringing a feast with him, they'll set up trestle tables in the warehouse, as they did a year earlier for a high-powered French delegation from Burgundy, come to see what all the fuss was about.

Clearly Jensen will spend on his beloved wines sooner than he'll spend on himself or his staff. The staff know this and are wryly affectionate about it—they, too, are loyal to the wines.

I poked about for an hour or two, dodging tarantulas and brooding about the San Andreas Fault a few hundred yards downhill, and then, before I left for the day, marshaled the winery staff outdoors for a photograph.

They shuffled out, looking sheepish, and stood in a stiff line for the camera. There were just nine of them, Jensen and his winemaker

Sara Steiner, winery manager Diana Vita and her assistant Judy Ferreira, cellar workers Abraham and Adolfo Corona and Jorge Reyes, utility worker Dave Larsen and Frédéric Magnien, son of the *propriétaire* of a small high-quality *domaine* in Burgundy, who was working at Calera to learn California ways (evidence of an interesting change in French sensibilities; until recently no Burgundian worth his *cuvée* would have deigned to assume anything could be learned from elsewhere. When young Magnien gets home he'll doubtless want to change everything, driving his father to distraction and terminally irritating the neighbors). I've looked often at this photograph since I took it, staring at the lineup, trying to see anything that would say, here are the people who produce one of the world's great wines. But it's no use. No one could possibly guess from the picture what these people do for a living. They're dressed in all-Americana: jeans, T-shirts, sweaters, sneakers, one or two pairs of boots, an overall. There's nothing glamorous about them, nothing particularly dull. If there are a few more Hispanic faces than would be the American norm, well, this is California. They could be a suburban bowling club, a law office out for a picnic, a busload of Presbyterian missionaries, anything.

I asked Jensen for an annotated reading on his staff.

Sara Steiner, Calera's winemaker, was a new employee when I met her, having arrived only four months earlier when the previous winemaker, Steve Doerner, left after fourteen years on the job "to pursue his own interests," as Jensen diplomatically put it. "She's new, but she's learning fast. She worked for six years for Haywood, up in Sonoma, a winery a little smaller than us who own their own zinfandel vineyard, and also make chardonnay, some sauvignon blanc and a little cabernet. She had never made pinot noir before she came here."

In many small wineries, especially those owned by wealthy urban refugees, dentists, lawyers or filmmakers like Francis Ford Coppola, the winemaker is the final arbiter of taste, the governor of the house style, the person who controls the decision-making process. Most were trained at Davis, then untrained on the job, before learning anew the manifold possibilities of the raw materials they work with.

In other wineries, whether massive operations like Gallo, where Julio Gallo is both co-owner and winemaker, or boutiques like Calera, where the obsession of the owner is what drives the whole operation, the winemaker is the quality-control expert, the person who uses chemistry to approximate the owner's art, the person who gives rhythm and timing to the owner's instinct.

In Steiner's case, because she was new, because of the oversize personality of Calera's owner and because she had arrived at a moment least opportune for a calm transition and a measured learning curve (just as the '91 pinot noir bottling was about to start and as the unexpectedly early and unexpectedly large 1992 crush arrived from the vineyards), she was using her time and her lab assays and tests not only to coddle and protect the existing wines but to learn to understand them.

It struck me that this must be very confusing. It also struck me that she was an exceptionally calm and orderly person, and even if she did have to keep many of her microbiological cultures in jars in the office fridge, she would be a good influence on the more mercurial personality of her proprietor.

Later she told me she had actually set out to be a vet, but developed an interest in plant biology along the way, and because she wanted to live in Sonoma she became a winemaker instead. Now she is neither a vet nor living in Sonoma, but is part custodian and part creator of some of the best wines being made anywhere.

Calera's most senior executive, winery manager Diana Vita, trained as an enologist and lab tech. She moved to the Central Coast area from Napa, where she had worked for several larger wineries as a chemical technician. Her husband's family had for many years owned a place on the ocean and they set up a small winemaking operation of their own. She is also raising two kids and commutes an hour to get to work in Calera every day, and it was a matter of some debate how long she would want to continue leading three or four lives. "She just showed up one day and asked if we needed someone to crank out assays," Jensen says. "She was going to be a two-days-a-week lab person, but now she runs the business. Ever since she's arrived she's been part of our tasting panel. She's been here for six years or so now, and she has a longer historical take on what we do and what our wines are like than Sara does for the moment.

"The three cellarmen are all Mexicans. They work the barrels, pressing and crushing, bottling and so on, they're great, they're the real reason for our success. They're hard working, smart, confident, a reliable bunch of guys.

"And then there's David Larsen, who is indispensable. He works half in the winery and half in the vineyards. He's our longest serving employee and also our oldest in age, older even than me. He also serves as watchman, as security guard, as handyman, is important during the crush, and then goes up and helps in the vineyards ... quite indispensable. He also does some of the engineering and the plumbing, as does Sara, who is good at that. We only get an electrician and plumber when we can't figure it out, which isn't often."

What about the vineyard crew, who weren't at the winery for my picture-taking?

"The manager is Jim Ryan, who has been with us since 1979. He took a college course in viticulture, grape farming, at CalPoly, now called California State University Polytechnic at San Luis Obispo, one of the major farm colleges in the state, along with UC Davis and Fresno State. There's also an assistant manager, Shawn Callahan, and recently we took on one of Jim's friends, Jerry Simmons, as a jack of all trades.

"Jesus Zendejas runs all our pruning and picking crews. People like working for him, so when we get into pruning he's got twenty people asking him to hire them, so he can get the three that he wants.

"In the course of the year we'll also bring other people in as necessary. In our case, our vineyard workers don't work in the winery — the three cellarmen pretty well handle it. Luckily this year we had young Frédéric with us, for without him we might not have managed, it was such a huge crop. He worked like a dog. The whole crew was going from seven in the morning until ten at night, for weeks, with not even Sundays off. After that was over, Sara scheduled a light day for one or two of them, or a day off for a couple of them. They were desperately in need of it."

❊　　❊　　❊

I walked back to my car, parked on the upper level road. It was late afternoon and a breeze like soft skin drifted across the landscape. It smelled of windblown dust and wild rosemary, with a faint trace of blue-gum eucalyptus, elusive and tantalizing. There was a beetle at the side of the road, its head down, butting at a small pebble, its black carapace gleaming in the slanting sun, its purpose inscrutable—*what will it do with the pebble when it gets it up the hill?* I looked back over the winery's angular roof to the landscape beyond, to the lengthening shadows on the distant slopes, black clefts in the golden hills. I felt a sudden slight melancholic tugging. It looked and smelled of home, of the hills between Fransch Hoek, where my heart is, and the golden fields of De Aar, where the African plains begin, the endless North that only ends in the Great Thirstland of the Kalahari Desert. Somewhere below, on the Cienega Road, a dog barked, and I thought I could faintly hear the lowing of cattle. It was a grand place, I thought, an appropriate place for a great wine and a grand obsession.

III

*In which the pinot noir makes its
appearance as the heartbreak grape,
and some thought is given to where
it came from and where it's going*

When it comes right down to it, all winemaking is similar—
it's the process of helping grapes ferment themselves into wine.

But, clearly, some methods of encouraging this process are better
than others. And some grapes make the job easier than others.

The pinot noir is one of the more difficult ones.

In those innocent days when gender descriptives were still
thought amusing, the pinot noir was called feminine—by which was
meant flighty, changeable, beguiling and seductive.

In the same vein, they called it the heartbreak grape because it
was so stubborn, so particular, so elusive, so damn difficult to get
right. And also because when it was at its best it made the most sublime wine of all. The heartbreak grape? You cannot break a heart
without having captured it first.

The greatest wines of Burgundy, which is where the greatest pinot
noirs have traditionally been elevated, are tantalizing, elusive, poetic,
thrilling. Even the most inspired red bordeaux, that cunning mixture
of cabernet and merlot, can't fill the head with spiced dreams quite
like the great burgundies. No other red wine can balance spice and

25

fruit so ... flirtatiously, can seem at once so ripe and fragile, so decadent and clean, so irresistible. And, it's fair to say, no other red wines
can drive the poor writer to such extravagant prolixity, as you can
plainly see from the foregoing, or from this overblown passage from
Oz Clarke: "The flavors of the great red Burgundies are sensuous,
often erotic, above rational discourse and beyond the powers of measured criticism as they flout the conventions in favor of something
rooted in emotions and passions too powerful to be taught, too
ancient to be meddled with."

Whew!

The heartbreak comes from dim memories of this greatness as producers all over the world, from the valleys of California or New
Zealand to the hearty plains of Australia or Argentina, contemplate
the thin, mean and insipid wines they have managed to concoct out of
the blessed pinot noir. If truth be told, many of the most insipid come
only a few meters from the great *domaines* of Burgundy itself, from
lesser slopes or lesser soil or lesser growers and producers taking
lesser care. And equal heartbreak from contemplation of attempts in
California to make wines approximating The Big Red One, heavy,
stultifying wines tasting of burned plum or, in the words of the British
wine writer Jancis Robinson, wines that "smelled unnervingly of
burned cabbage."

The capricious nature of pinot noir in the bottle reflects a similar
flightiness in the vine itself. Pinot noir mutates if you give it a cross
look, seemingly out of pure spite. It's a master of the genetic dance.
It's also very old, and no one can any longer say which is the "original" clone; there was pinot noir already planted in the Burgundy area
when the Romans pushed gingerly into the deep interior of Gaul—
Pliny describes it, in an early bout of critical purple. And Burgundy
is now thick with clones of all qualities, after many attempts to fight
off the viruses and fungi to which the variety is so prone, blast it.
Some "burgundies" are made with what probably isn't pinot noir at
all, but *pinot droit*, an upright clone similar to many invented in
California by the techies of Davis, which bears more fruit than the
traditional *pinot fin*. There are supposed to be three hundred and

sixty-five clones of pinot noir now growing along the tight little ridge of Burgundy. Well, that's a neat number—others say there are two hundred or a thousand. And, considering that each clone would affect the wine differently because of its particular genetic structure, it's easy to see why this is "a minx of a vine," an exasperating variety for growers, winemakers and critics, as well as the humble wine drinker. This welter of wines, this passel of pinots, makes standard-bearing and standard-keeping a thankless task. It's further compli-cated by the pinot noir vine's tendency to degenerate and to die early, sometimes decades before it should. And complicated yet again by pinot noir's notorious reluctance to travel to new climes, where its "feminine" allure seems to pine away into old-maidish rectitude.

That, at least, was the thought a decade or so ago. The problem was, winemakers in these new climes got it all wrong. They plunked the vine down into the arid heat of the California plains, where the poor thing became sunburned and petulant. As a consequence, the early American pinot noirs had size and weight, but lacked subtlety, finesse or much character.

If that wasn't enough, the pinot noir is also an early budder with sluggish secondary growth, so spring frosts are deadly. Some years the vines stubbornly refuse to set fruit, the flowers simply withering instead of turning to precious grapes. No one seems to know why.

The pinot noir grape is as capricious as the vine. Its petulance comes from its thin skin. It needs regular sun to ripen, but will quickly overripen if the sun gets too hot. On the other hand, it can't cope with too much rain. It will swell and burst and rot if it gets too wet at harvest time. It's also an early ripener; the longer the grapes can stay on the vine the more complex the resulting wines, but the tendency to rot in the rain and to burn in the sun greatly elevates the risk. And if it gets too ripe it will lose its fruit flavors and potential for grandeur.

Color, flavors and tannins are precariously balanced in the pinot noir. Sometimes, the vine seems naturally to produce grapes rich in tannins and anthocyanins and a deep ruby color. More often, it will produce an insipid rosé the color of antique brick. Climate can effect this swing. So can weather, soil, elevation, sunshine, moisture, pruning, picking, fermentation, filtering and a dozen other things, apparently up to and including the phases of the moon and the moods of the winemaker.

To the wine drinker, pinot noirs are robust, vigorous and explosive. But to the winemaker, they are fragile, prone to spoilage, delicate. The making of pinot noir requires—demands—a deftness of touch that was generally thought to be alien to the California character. Got an A-plus in enological studies? The pinot noir won't care. As Steve Doerner once put it, "Since pinot noir starts out as a delicate wine without a strong backbone, every time you do something to it, you strip more of the body out of it. So, if you're striving for a rich, complex wine, the less you handle it the closer you'll come." With pinot noir, structure is easy to get. It is subtleness, perfume and richness that are the difficult things. Because of this ... elusiveness ... the making of pinot noir becomes an overriding passion and obsession. Its nature remains a mystery, and it remains the wine that most serious winemakers want to make—and most serious winemakers want to drink.

And there's one other problem with it. It changes, the fickle thing, even in the bottle. Josh Jensen, when he's holding a tasting for important clients, likes to open a bottle the night before to see how it's "performing." This is not a matter of variation between bottles of the same batch, which plagues all winemakers, but that pinot noir is always restless, constantly undergoing changes.

So while everyone recognizes a great pinot noir when they come across one, pinot noir has no single universally accepted flavor or style. It can be pitiful to watch wine writers struggling for acceptable comparatives. Without trying you can find pinot noir variously tasting of fresh wild strawberries (or, more often, raspberries), of damsons or other plums, of black cherries, of vanilla and butter and violets on the delicate side, of pepper and all-spice and truffles on the robust side, and of "earthiness," sometimes off-puttingly described as "farmyard" or "barnyard" or game, or even rotten vegetables. One eminent writer, despairingly, wrote that it "smelled like shit," and meant it, approvingly. Of course, presumably he meant the sweeter odor of the cow and he was likely thinking of hay in a summer barn, but I still think he should have tried again.

Joseph Ward, writing in *Condé Nast Traveler* in September 1992, said of pinot noir that it was "quicksilver to cabernet's iron," a nice phrase. Joel Fleishman, wine *amateur* and Duke University's vice president, wrote in *Vanity Fair* in August 1991: "At their best, pinot noirs are the most romantic of wines, with so voluptuous a perfume, so sweet an edge, and so powerful a punch that, like falling in love, they make the blood run hot and the soul wax embarrassingly poetic." (Well, at least he admitted it.)

The great California winemaker André Tchelistcheff, who can be forgiven the solecism because of his old-fashioned European courtliness, once called pinot noir "the wonderful aroma of the inside of a kid glove worn by a young woman." This will not do much for its marketing among female drinkers, but unreconstructed romantic males can see what he means.

Could pinot noir be made to work in California? Tchelistcheff, always good for a quote, once said he'd made a "superb pinot noir [at Beaulieu in Napa], but I don't know how I did it and I was never able to do it again."

Most California pinot noirs are still hot and simplistic, one-dimensional wines; when you hear a California winemaker defend himself by saying he's trying for "a California style," you can be sure he means he was unable to duplicate what he knew in his heart was the real thing. Still, this defensiveness is forgivable. For years Californians smarted from the condescension of the lofty Burgundians. That the French, secure in their centuries-old Gallic superiority, were able to be snottily polite only made it worse—the French have always been able to say "Yes, but ..." better than anyone. Typical was the haughty Lalou Leroy, co-proprietor of the mighty Domaine de la Romanée-Conti, who, when confronted with a superb pinot noir from Chalone, sniffed, *"Oui, mais c'est chaud."* She later deigned to be "impressed" by Oregon and remembered an Eyrie Vineyards pinot noir that was *"intéressant," "mais assez léger."*

Well, this is all gone now. Madame may sniff, but the more fore-sighted Burgundians are sending their sons to America and Australia to learn the new ways of doing things. Just as the Californians and the Oregonians learned a hard-won lesson: go back to Burgundy to learn how it's done.

And so, having done precisely that, Josh Jensen joined with Acacia (Chalone), Zaca Mesa, Sanford, Belvedere, Iron Horse and Château Bouchaine in Pinot Noir America, a producers' association, when they began to make wines as rich and as satisfying as the best of the Old World, wines that smelled of cherries and ripe plums, of chocolate and leather, with the same beguiling sweet silk of the great-est red burgundies, those of the Domaine de la Romanée-Conti or those of Henri Jayer in Vosne-Romanée and Nuits St-Georges.

Our bottle of wine—any bottle of wine—can have its lineage tracked to ancient times, through thousands of generations of producers and consumers. No one knows how far back the vine goes. Brillat-Savarin, the gourmet and critic, is typical of many in France who assume that wine was made in the far mists of time. "There are only two things that separate man from the beasts," he wrote. "Fear of the future, and a desire for fermented liquors." Wine is mentioned in many texts of ancient Mesopotamia, of ancient Egypt and of Gaul. The Epic of Gilgamesh has many stanzas singing the praises of wine; so does the Song of Solomon. There were vineyards in Sumeria, in Assyria and in ancient Greece. Primitive grape presses, fermentation tanks and treading platforms antedating Christ by millennia have been found in the Caucasus between the Black and Caspian seas. From there it's fair to say that the Caucasians took grapevines with them wherever they went. From what we now call Syria and Lebanon the Phoenicians distributed grapes throughout the Mediterranean. So did their successors, the Greeks, who, upon first being exposed to Italy, called it the Land of Vines, the same name given by the Vikings to North America two thousand years later, when confronted with the native *vitis labrusca* (with which, alas, they attempted to make wine—and still do, in places, producing gallons of mediocre wine with a pronounced flavor, rather mysteriously called "foxy" by wine people). The vine arrived in France more than two thousand years ago from the Transcaucasus by way of the Euphrates valley, Egypt and Greece. Probably the colonizers from ancient Ionia first grew grapes at the mouth of the Rhône, but it was the Romans who first planted vines in the interior of "that barbarous place." And after the collapse of the Roman empire, the wine business was essentially saved by the Christians, who needed it for their mass; monastic Christian orders were among the first to set out vineyards in what are now some of the most highly regarded wine-growing regions of Germany, France, Austria and the Danube valley.

The California wine industry, which began in the 1870s, induced largely by Italian and East European immigrants, proved short-lived—rye whisky was still the American alcoholic beverage of choice. The years following the repeal of Prohibition produced little wine of interest, though Davis was quietly doing its work and the Gallos were laying the foundation for their extraordinary dominance of American winemaking. It wasn't until the 1970s that California noticed that it was producing wines of great character and complexity in numerous small pockets around the state—the Russian River Valley, the Green Valley, Napa and Sonoma and Santa Barbara and Monterey, though the chilly fogs in Monterey Bay made it hard to ripen grapes. And in the late 1970s, with the famous Paris Tasting that pitted the best Americans against the best Europeans, to Europe's chagrin and America's triumph, the world at last accepted California as one of the premier wine regions on the planet.

They made wonderful robust cabernets. They produced merlots, chardonnays, sauvignon blancs, even zinfandels of quality. Only the pinot noir eluded them. By the end of the '70s the Heartbreak Grape was still regarded as the Last Hurdle for California winemakers.

Vitis vinifera is only one of about forty grape species in the world. Almost all of them are deciduous, highly susceptible to fungi and parasites, needful of considerable heat and sunlight and—perhaps most importantly—able to crossbreed spontaneously. There are now literally thousands of vinifera varieties and, if you count clones, as the viticulturalists call stable mutations, thousands more.

You can make wines from all of them. Poor wines, mostly. Only a handful—fewer than fifty—of the great vinifera catalogue will make wines worth drinking. But what a litany of names! The chardonnay, gamay and pinot noir of Burgundy. The sauvignons—cabernet and blanc—of Bordeaux. The riesling of Germany, the chenin blanc of the Loire and the viognier and syrah of the Rhône. The sémillon, which makes the silken sweetness of sauternes; the muscat of the Crimea and southern Spain—I have a particular fondness for the muscat, because from it my ancestors made the succulent sweet wine called Constantia, which was drunk to much acclaim at the court of Napoleon.

In much of the winegrowing world, grape varieties have been matched over the centuries to *terroir*, as the French call their little micro-pockets. In many places, such as Bordeaux, no one variety will do and a blend has been found to do best. Few in the Old World ever listed the grape varieties on their labels, which seemed designed rather to satisfy local pride and parochial politics than enlighten the drinker. Nor was it strictly necessary. Everyone in the region already knew what the grape variety was. And, later, the use of these varieties was mandated by law—you can't call a white burgundy by that name unless it's made entirely of chardonnay. Therefore, while the wines were well known, few consumers knew the grape. Who had heard of the palomino of sherry, the syrah and the elegant, flowery viognier of the Rhône, the merlot, malbec and petit verdot of Bordeaux or, until recently, the gewürztraminer of Alsace? It was only in the New World that winemakers, no longer bound by tradition (because tradition, by definition, is accreted and not invented) began to label their wines with the grape varietal. The Old World is beginning to follow suit (the new trendiness of viognier in California, for instance, has persuaded the handful of French producers to declare its existence on their labels too) and this has done more to simplify the pleasures of wine than almost anything else.

However, there's still plenty of room for disagreement among ampelographers, grape specialists. America's zinfandel is the most prominent example—is it really a primitivo from Italy or something else entirely? Is Spain's pedro ximenez, used for making sherry, really a riesling from Germany? Does anyone but the nationalist zealots care?

The Romans were wine drinkers and arbiters of taste, and established the vineyards that still endure as the greatest in France: on the low spit of gravel, limestone and clay between the Atlantic and the Gironde near Bordeaux, on the chalky hills of Champagne, in the flinty Loire valley and in Burgundy, on an undistinguished and commonplace limestone ridge less than thirty kilometers long, called the Côte d'Or, which is remarkable only for its unremarkableness. Still, the Côte d'Or is the heart of Burgundy, and has produced wines of superlative quality. Samuel Johnson was one of many wine drinkers who fell in love with the wines of this small ridge. He once confided that he couldn't remember much about the first time he had made love; he couldn't remember the date or the woman's name, and could only faintly picture her face and her body. "But the wine! The wine, by god, was a Chambertin!" (My own view of this anecdote, having read contemporary descriptions of Johnson, was that the Chambertin was the only reason the young woman agreed to be seduced in the first place.)

An even more remarkable thing about this unremarkable ridge is the fact that some few small parcels on its slopes yield up superlative wines and others do not, and though soil and subsoil and temperature and humidity and *climat*—the elevation above the fogs, the aspect or slope of the parcel, its orientation towards the sun and the prevailing winds—have all been exhaustively analyzed, the central mystery remains. With one more added: two growers on the same parcel will make very different wines.

Burgundy and Bordeaux winemaking differ not only because of grape varieties and climate, but because of history and politics. The reason many Bordeaux wines are produced on substantial estates is because Eleanor of Aquitaine, when she held the region, imposed on it the English system of primogeniture. The estate generally went to the eldest son, and so was kept intact. By contrast, although Burgundy was once one of the greatest duchies of France, it was broken up by the last of the Bourbon kings and its remaining great landholdings, those of the church, were scattered by Napoleon. As a result, it now has a curiously rustic air—there are none of the great châteaux of the Loire here, nor even the great merchant houses so prominent along the Médoc. Instead, there has been endless subdivision of land. It's still commonplace for four sons to inherit a small property and each to jealously guard his half hectare. For a grower in Burgundy, three acres is a large property, and it would be larger than most of his neighbors'.

Therefore, the Burgundians have attempted a complex grading of fields; each field, and even each part of a field, has been classified and inserted into a hierarchy that is codified and cast into law. There are a hundred or more appellations in Burgundy, many of them referring to a minute parcel of a specific vineyard, and built into these allowable appellations is a classification by quality (into Grands Crus, Premiers Crus, Appellations Communales and, at the bottom, simply Bourgogne). The differences on the label can be minute, but the variance in quality absolute. Many villages, for reasons of status and therefore income, have attached their names to famous vineyards and the results can be confusing and apparently contradictory— Chassagne-Montrachet can be wine of varying quality from anywhere in a big commune; Chevalier-Montrachet can only be wine from one tiny, if famous, vineyard. Nor can the human factor be codified. A wine from a particular field in a particular commune in a particular year could still have been made by any of six or seven winemakers. *Monopoles*, or whole vineyards, in the hands of one grower are rare exceptions. Of those *monopoles*, the eighteen or so hectares of the Domaine de la Romanée-Conti are the most prestigious and the wines produced there—Romanée-Conti, La Tâche, Richebourg and Romanée-St.-Vivant—are the most coveted red wines in the world, now fetching prices out of reach of all but the very wealthy or the completely besotted. The vines are perfectly sited in limestone soil above the village of Vosne-Romanée, but this doesn't begin to explain the extraordinary opulence, the velvety warmth, the complexity and spiciness of the wines. Romanée-Conti has always been the model, the grail, for Josh Jensen. On that *monopole* lies the real origin of our bottle, in reality as well as fancy, as we shall see.

Burgundian styles vary over time. Historically, they were deep and dark. About fifteen years ago there was a swing to much lighter wines, paler, with less depth of flavor and less ability to mature; and more recently, the start of another swing, back to richness and complexity. Josh Jensen's view is that perfect pinot noir is one that is perfectly balanced on that cusp and is neither one nor the other. It should be light and delicate as well as opulent, and complex and subtle above all.

There are other complications to understanding burgundy. Burgundian winemakers are not usually, or even typically, grape growers, although that is changing fast as the growers challenge the power of the merchants of Beaune, called *negociants* or sometimes *negociants-éleveurs* (people who sell, but who also "elevate" or "educate" the wines — that is, people who believe their judgment is paramount).

Traditionally, most of Burgundy's growers were farmers who grew the grapes and pressed them, and in the musty depths of their old cellar basements they'd keep ten or eleven barrels where they'd store the new raw wine. Then Louis Latour or Joseph Drouhin or one of the Jaffelin Frères or another of the great *negociants* would come by and taste it, and if they liked it and met the farmer's price they'd buy it from him, all his barrels of raw, newly fermented wine. If his patch were entitled to the name Gevrey-Chambertin Grand Cru, then along with the barrels the merchant would get the green tags that allowed him to bottle and sell that many bottles of Gevrey-Chambertin Grand Cru.

In the last twenty years this has been changing. The 1980s brought a horrid inflation in the prices of burgundies. As prices on the open market soared, criticism swelled also — criticism of the poor quality of much of the wine. The powerful backlash that resulted persuaded some of the younger growers — and a few older ones — to assert themselves. They wanted a better living for themselves, and to produce something they could be proud of. They began to call themselves "harvesting proprietors" and began to finish the winemaking themselves, marketing and selling their own produce. Frédéric Magnien, the young man who spent four months with Calera, is the son of such a proprietor. As a consequence, the great and arrogant *negociants* lost considerable power and in some years, much to the malicious glee of the growers, they now actually have trouble getting enough juice. All this has made good burgundy harder and harder to find and buy, but cheaper and more interesting because of it.

And one more thing has happened: as California began to produce better wines, the small Burgundians, lacking the prejudices of their betters, began to understand that there was now real competition coming from the New World. The best ones welcomed it; the others whined.

The Californians, for their part, moved closer to the sensibility of Burgundy. As Josh Jensen put it, "There are many growers who don't make wine here. In fact, most California wine comes from farmers who sell their crop to whoever comes along, to five different wineries if those wineries pay their price. We at Calera do that with our Central Coast wines, which in the drought years have been as much as eighty percent of our production. We try to find some good pinot noir and chardonnay vineyards and just buy their fruit."

But his heart isn't there. "I'm a Burgundian. That's my perspective. Control of grapes, the climate from which they come and the soil in which they are grown, is paramount to me. I must have my own vineyards to make great wine."

IV

*In which the maker of our bottle
of wine goes to Burgundy to pick
grapes, and to learn some
pre-nineteenth-century technology*

The man who made our bottle of wine grew up across the Bay
from San Francisco. His mother's family owned a lumber company in
the Pacific Northwest; his father, Stephen Fairchild Jensen, was born
in Seattle in 1910 and paid his way through dental school by driving
trucks for his cousins' Seattle seafood company. He was, from all
accounts, a better dentist than truck driver; his most vivid moment as
a trucker came when he tried and failed to make a turn one frosty
morning, spilling a truckload of fresh oysters over Highway 99.

Before the war he practiced dentistry for a number of years in
Shanghai, where he married Josh's mother, Jasmine Eddy, and
where Josh's older brother and sister were born. After Navy service
in the war, he set up his dental practice in the Bay area town of
Orinda, where he and Josh's mother still live. Along the way he
fished and hunted, bred black Labrador hunting dogs and, with his
wife, raised quarter horses.

Wine, however, was never part of the household's daily life; it was
never served with meals, the family had no cellar and they stored
what few bottles they acquired in their quonset-hut barn, along with

the cow, horses and a pig—much to the amusement of Dr. George Selleck, who had given them the wine.

It was Selleck, a dentist colleague and friend of Jensen père, who first introduced young Josh to wine and could be said to be the founding father of our bottle. Jensen recalls him with affection: "It was in the late 1940s that George thought my dad should start learning about wine and bought him some German wines. It was these my dad stored in our quonset hut. I remember tasting them with George. He had a major collection of wine, a great cellar, and with it an incredible palate for and knowledge of wine. He was a connoisseur of the first rank, a man who knew everyone in the wine business in California. Later, at dinners at his house, I progressed to bordeaux and burgundies."

It was Selleck who first pointed out to young Josh that the wine world could be divided into two distinct and irreconcilable factions, passionate Bordelais and romantic Burgundians, though Selleck himself could (and did) swing both ways and had wonderful collections of each. He was one of the founders of the San Francisco Food & Wine Society and was the first dentist president of the Society of Medical Friends of Wine. In the '40s and '50s he served as one of five judges at the California State Fair Wine Competition, then the only competition of any consequence in America. The other four judges were André Tchelistcheff, Philip Wagner, the winemaker and author from the east coast, the eminent Professor Maynard Amerine of UC Davis and Dr. Salvatore Lucia of San Francisco.

Amerine once told Josh about a blind tasting hosted by another member of their group of post-Prohibition San Francisco wine pioneers, in which everyone was given eight glasses of red wine and asked to identify them. The host appeared to have stumped them when, as Amerine recounted it, George suddenly got that twinkle in his eye, re-tasted the eight glasses and wrote out his guesses. He alone recognized that it was all Château Latour, eight different vintages, and he correctly identified six of the eight. Amerine believed it one of the greatest feats of blind tasting he'd ever seen.

Selleck was twice decorated by the French government, as Chevalier du Mérite Agricole, and Commandeur du Mérite Agricole, for his knowledge of French wine and food. "He was a true connoisseur and bon vivant in the best sense of both terms, and his joie de vivre, expertise and generosity were and remain an inspiration for me," Jensen wrote in a memorial much later.

Josh put in a few years at Yale and then went to Oxford to do a Masters in Anthropology, for reasons he now forgets—little of what he learned there stuck with him except, for our purposes, his further education into the mysteries of burgundy.

He spent more time, in truth, in a boat than a classroom. Although bigger than the norm for an oarsman, he did make the Oxford team and competed in the annual Boat Race against Cambridge at Henley, earning himself a mention in the *Guinness Book of World Records* as the heaviest man ever to have done so. He enjoyed rowing and the Oxford team of the time, unusually, stayed together and competed for the Grand Challenge Cup at Henley in 1967, eventually losing in the semifinals to the East Germans.

Oxford was the first time in his life he drank wine every day. Not necessarily in college, though at every Oxford college there's a High Table at which the faculty and heads of college eat and drink wines from formidable cellars. Jensen was not High Table material, but there were plenty of good restaurants around the city and he could afford to eat out frequently. Much later, at a Vinexpo show in Bordeaux, Jensen met the eminent Jean Michel Cazes, a star in the wine business, proprietor of Château Lynch Bages and the manager and operator of a number of other Bordeaux wineries. "I told him that when I was a student at Oxford, Lynch Bages was my regular dinner wine and he was pretty surprised. But then, in a restaurant, you'd maybe pay seven or eight dollars, or ten, for a bottle of Lynch Bages or its equivalent. In the sixties, you really could drink those wines. You didn't need to be a millionaire to drink great wines. Wine was just an everyday thing.

"I don't really remember when the light went on, but on it clicked, and suddenly I realized, hey, wine is a part of life, not just something you have at Christmas dinner or when you put a tuxedo on. It's part of the richness of everyday life."

It was there, at Oxford, and Château Lynch Bages notwithstanding, that he gave his heart to Burgundy.

"I was at Oxford for two and a half years, and I suppose that during that time I had wine every night with dinner. And after a while, I found that I liked the ones called Gevrey-Chambertin and Nuits St-Georges or Vosne-Romanée more than I liked the ones called Château this or Château that.

"I love a great bordeaux. When I have a great bordeaux I say to myself, this is a great wine, this has everything, color, intensity, flavor, balance, acid. But when I taste a great burgundy I say wow, I'm in love! It's very different. It's a visceral, emotional response. And I've seen Bordelais react the same way, but in reverse."

He was still pretty hazy on the geography of Burgundy, but not at all hazy in knowing that the academic life was not for him. He didn't want to be a professor. So he set off for the Côte d'Or.

"I knew I really liked drinking the wine. I wanted to see if I liked the life, the work, the elbow-grease end of it. Could I make my life doing this?"

He set off in the summer of 1969.

He knew the language, sort of. "I'd taken French at school and college for five years, so I could read and write beautifully. But I couldn't speak it. I couldn't order a cup of coffee properly—that wasn't part of the teaching of languages in this country, at least back then. So I learned to speak by living there."

Where was "there"?

George Selleck had shared a few precious bottles of Romanée-Conti with the young Jensen, and had told him something of the lore and the prestige of the place, "so I knew that was the best place to learn winemaking—why not go for the very best there is? So I simply went there, I showed up one day and knocked on the door. 'Do you need pickers?' I asked.

"'Yeah,' they said, 'come back in about a week, what's your name?'

"They seemed quite surprised to see me. They didn't have a lot of Americans volunteering to pick grapes."

The great *domaines* of Burgundy draw their field workers from several sources. The harvest in Burgundy is in September, stretching through to October, and the first category of pickers are French students, who do it to make a little cash; they start in the south, in Provence, and follow the harvest north, Burgundy being one of the last, before Champagne. The second source of help are people from the surrounding villages, wives of the workers, wives of the cellarmen, neighbors. This is the traditional source of all harvest labor. The third source are people who simply love the work. Josh Jensen remembers a fellow picker at Romanée-Conti in 1970 who worked in a bank in Dijon. "He took his vacation every year at harvest time and worked like a pig all through harvest. I still remember this twenty years later, it astonished me so much, because that is hard, hard work. It's often cold and raining, but he loved it. It was a great change for him." The fourth source are the gypsies. "They're the equivalent of our Mexicans, immigrant migrant field workers. These guys work so fast! You try to put a student with soft hands out there and these guys will be at the end of the row before the student has picked the first two vines." Jensen himself was part of a small but not unimpressive fifth category — students of the business.

Even in the high-margin wineries of the Grands Crus, the harvest, the *vendange*, is not at all a grim industrial occasion; Burgundy, after all, has been known as the stomach of France, and picking is an occasion for merriment and singing, festivity and food. The winery lodges and feeds its pickers, who take their meals in the fields, weather permitting. Breakfasts can be sardines, bread and red wine. Lunch is pot au feu or a cassoulet, soups, fish dishes, with pots of red wine, bread and great hunks of cheese.

Jensen was hired at the Domaine de la Romanée-Conti by one of the great figures of French winemaking, the *maître de chai* of the *domaine*, André Noblet. Noblet presided over the winemaking at Romanée-Conti for many years, a great, hulking bear of a figure (he had been a prominent rugby player as a youth) with twinkling eyes and a shrewd appreciation of man and nature. He had wanted to be a printer, but was persuaded back to the calling of his father by M. Leroy, one of the proprietors of Romanée-Conti. When Josh first met him he was near the end of his long career, but at the height of his knowledge and authority. He'd been born in the village itself, knew everyone, had the confidence of his employers, made the best wines in the world—he was perfectly placed to teach the young Californian what he needed to know.

"The really nice thing about the best wineries," Jensen recalls, "is that they're like the best chefs. They really don't have secrets. It always bugs me when I hear someone ask a chef, how did you make this sauce? And he says, 'That's a secret.' Those are the small individuals with little knowledge and small talent, because they're afraid they won't be able to stay ahead of their competitors. The real talents are happy to share all they know, because they know that next year they'll be creating something new and even better. They're teachers. André Noblet was very much like that."

Not everyone in Burgundy, however, was "like that," and Jensen encountered French xenophobia in his second harvest as a picker at Romanée-Conti.

"After the '70 crush was over I told André I'd like to work in the cellar for the following harvest, then go back to the States.

"'Sure,' he said, 'no problem.'

"I pushed him: 'Do you have to ask anybody else about this?'

"And he said, 'No, I'm the *maître de chai* and I don't have to ask anybody.'

"I checked with him four times during the year—I *can* work in the cellar, right? I'd learned what I could in the vineyard. And the first year I'd hung around for a week after the harvest, picking up what I could. Also, in the mornings before we went into the fields I'd help punch-down the fermenting cap in the tanks. It's called the *pigeage* and you do it with your feet in the old way, you just get into the tank and push the cap down. There had been a huge crop that year and they'd destemmed the bunches just for space reasons—mostly they fermented their wines with all the stems attached. This punching down is hard work. I'd help in the morning and then, after we'd finished the picking, I'd help with the evening punch-down too, asking questions all the time, learning, and André liked this. I was a good worker, in the same way young Frédéric Magnien is for me—he works like a dog, a fabulous worker.

"So I showed up for the '71 harvest and reported to the cellar as planned. And there I ran afoul of one of the members of one of the families that owned, and still owns, Romanée-Conti. The *domaine* is owned by two families, the de Villaine family, the most prominent of whom is Aubert, a friend of mine since those days, and the Leroy family. The second or third day I was in the cellar shoveling grapes into tanks and punching down and doing other cellar work and I spotted old M. de Villaine, Aubert's father, and old M. Leroy talking. Leroy's daughter, Lalou, and Aubert were called in and were casting nervous glances in my direction. Finally, to his embarrassment, they sent Aubert over to tell me that M. Leroy didn't want me in the winery.

"I said I'd checked with André a dozen times, but it was no use.

"'I'm sorry,' Aubert said, 'he just doesn't want you here. He wants you in the fields.'

"'I don't do fields,' I said, 'I did that last year.'

"I went on working.

"Then Lalou came over. 'We think you should go out in the fields,' she said.

"'I don't think so, no thank you,' I said.

"Finally her father came over and said, 'Well, we think you'd be better off in the fields.'

"'If I can't work here in the cellar I'm not working for you in this harvest,' I said.

"'Well, sorry you feel that way,' he said.

"'Okay, I'll check out right away,' I said, and I went to my friend's place. It was pretty uncomfortable. But out I went."

Jensen has maintained friendly relations with Aubert de Villaine ever since, but never warmed to the remarkable Lalou, one of the great characters of Burgundy. "I've preferred to stay out of her way. I'd rather not have anything to do with her."

Lalou, meanwhile, went on to become the public face of the DRC, as Romanée-Conti is known to the trade; she was, among other things, its official sales agent. Lalou was (and is), to put it politely, a forceful personality. She was often seen in the *chai* in her chic trousers and smart little bomber jackets, issuing orders hither and yon. But she knew her stuff: Gault & Millau, the French restaurant critics, have written of her encyclopedic knowledge of wines (though their judgment might have been colored by the meals she served to France's gastronomic elite, including themselves, every year—perhaps her friendship with the great chef Jean Troisgros didn't hurt either). It was always assumed that Lalou bullied the quiet and scholarly Aubert, though she used to say of him, "We take all the important decisions together, although we don't always agree." As it happens, Jensen picked the right person for a friend: Lalou, otherwise known as Mme Bize-Leroy, was fired as DRC's sales agent after a long legal wrangle and wound up on the losing side of a twelve-million-dollar lawsuit against the property and the de Villaine family. So Aubert, in the end, refused to be bullied.

Jensen is still puzzled why he was ejected. It wasn't for the "secrets"—even had there been any, André Noblet would tell them to all and sundry. "I think it was difficult, and different, for them to have an American come over. They didn't have any secrets, it wasn't that. They just didn't want anyone poking around."

In a way, Jensen had already learned what he needed. Not so much in the fields, but afterwards. The pickers never got to drink DRC wines. They would eat and drink endlessly—hunks of bread, hunks of cheese, hunks of sausage and a big tub of wine, "so we'd been drinking wine all day long to mellow out while we were picking in the rain." This was wine they made specifically for the pickers at harvest time, at its best merely acceptable.

"By the time I left I'd learned quite a bit by watching. And because André couldn't speak English, and the DRC would get a lot of American business people coming through, André would bring me out to translate. And while I was translating, I was tasting. When André got some big shots in for a tasting he'd haul all the great wines out—he'd taste all the barrels of one vintage and then all the barrels of the next, and then he'd start bringing out the bottles. The retailers from New Jersey would ask, 'What date did they pick this? When did they do that?' And I'd ask André and translate, and meantime I'd get to taste and taste and taste these wines, these sublime wines, and I'd be learning all the time."

Between the '70 and the '71 vintages Jensen was either living in Paris or traveling through Bordeaux, up to Champagne, down the Rhône valley, and back to Burgundy. He'd spend time in Burgundy, and would stop by to see André and be asked to do another translation, and have a taste of this or that *domaine* wine.

He picked for a while at the Domaine Dujac, whose owner, Jacques Seysses, became one of his closest friends, and in nearby Condrieu on the Rhône, where he was paid in bottles of viognier wine. "You can't in any case survive financially picking grapes. I was using some money I inherited. I wasn't staying at five-star hotels either. I stayed with friends a lot. My car was a Citroën Deux Chevaux delivery van. It cost me forty dollars. I drove it for a year and sold it for forty dollars at the end. But I did spend good money at restaurants. At that time, for twenty dollars you could have a good meal for one person in most three-star restaurants."

He'd already bought all the French wine texts, particularly the Burgundy texts, and was plowing through them to figure out what else he needed to know to actually make the kinds of wine he liked to drink.

"I'd pretty much decided by then. I liked the work, I liked the people, I liked the product, I liked the art of it, I liked the challenge of trying to make something that everybody at that time said just could not be done in the U.S. I was *ready*."

What he learned was a style of winemaking that he was to take back to the United States, there to find himself in complete opposition to the prevailing American mode, which was high-tech, dominated by chemists. When he first went to Burgundy he'd been shocked at how little processing or handling was done to the grapes. "I mean, basically they pick the grapes and they put them in tanks, and then they go away for a couple of days, and then they come back to see if it's started fermenting yet." He kept looking around eagerly, waiting for the magic procedures, the great secrets, the enological legerdemain, to begin. "But there was no hocus pocus. And here's the secret: the making of great pinot noir is like making a Model T Ford, just a few simple steps.

"These are the greatest wines in the world and they are made by the most bare-bones production methods—grapes, wooden casks, bottles. Not even a filter, never mind a centrifuge. This wasn't space-age technology. It wasn't even nineteenth-century technology.

"I was absolutely entranced."

A few months later, Jensen went home to make our bottle of wine.

V

*In which our winemaker returns
to California to apply what he
has learned and buys an eyedropper
and a bottle of hydrochloric acid*

osh Jensen returned to California in late 1971 ready, as he put it, "to go for broke," to begin the adventure, to start making the great wine he knew he was capable of. His nostrils, and his dreams, were filled with the aromas of great Burgundian pinot noirs, and with his inner eye he could see his cellars, the serried ranks of barrels, the heady fizz of fermentation, his bottles of California pinot noir on the glossy pages of the most prestigious publications. At that point, pinot noirs of finesse and quality were nowhere to be found in the New World. Worse (or better, from Jensen's point of view), everybody who was anybody had concluded that the lively and capricious pinot noir just wouldn't adapt to the crude California sun, or would adapt only sullenly, grudgingly yielding up mediocre wines. Winemaker after winemaker had tried it, the making of great "burgundy," only to see the sun burn the fruit and the color from the grape, and all the complexity, subtlety (and pure fun) just leached away. The heart-break grape, indeed. The pragmatic professors at Davis declared the pinot noir unsuitable for California, and urged farmers to cut their losses and turn to something more tolerant of harsh conditions, like

the cabernet sauvignon, the muscular and phlegmatic grape of
Bordeaux, or the syrah, the toast of the Rhône, or the zinfandel,
native to who knows where, which was undergoing something of a
renaissance at the time (or a fad, depending on your point of view).

"I thought I'd shoot the works on one big gamble," Jensen says now.
"Can't grow pinot noir here, eh? No good in California and never will
be, eh? I figured as long as I'm gambling, I might as well not hedge my
bets. Go for broke. Go for the big one. I planted all pinot noir."

Did anyone notice that he was ignoring their advice?

"Yes, not only my family, who were my investors, but everyone
else as well. Everybody thought I was crazy."

In the cellars of the Domaine de la Romanée-Conti, whenever
Jensen poked about, asking questions, asking why they did this,
didn't do that, shouldn't they be doing the other, he'd ask again and
again: Why are these wines so special? And they'd shrug and say, ah,
it's the soil, it's the limestone in the soil ...

He wasn't the first American to run up against the French insistence on the primacy of soil as a determinant in the quality of wine. It
was one reason the French were so slow to accept the possibility of
superior California wines in the first place—they believed that nothing could replace the native genius of the soils of France. At
Romanée-Conti they'd simply point to the limestone ridge behind
them, where the crumbly rock had decomposed over the millennia
and was being brought down by erosion to the deeper soils of the
lower slopes. The crushed limestone, combined with the richer marl
a third of the way up the slope, gives their wines their particular flavors. Not just at Romanée-Conti either. Whenever serious California
winemakers prodded the French, the response they'd get back
invariably included the words *climat* and *terroir*, the rough French
equivalents of what some Americans were calling microclimate—
some sort of fictive combination of moisture, soil, weather, slope, elevation and sunshine. But what the French really seemed to believe
in, when push came to shove, was soil. This despite the unpublicized
fact that Romanée-Conti itself constantly "improves" its soil with rich

imported loam (perhaps the most celebrated soil-improvement program in history was the hundred and fifty wagon-loads of turf spread on its vineyards in the year 1749).

Jensen came to share the French belief in soil. Nothing else seemed to account for the daily miracles he was tasting at the DRC.

"Remember, whenever I asked what it was that made their wines so special, they'd say limestone soil. So ... for me ... limestone.

"People love to have theories about where quality comes from. For Francis Mahoney at Carneros, it's clones, the perfect vine. For others, it's the perfect barrel—say, three-quarters Tronçais and one-quarter Allier oak. Others think it's the perfect yeast, while others think it's the combination of malolactic and non-malolactic fermentations. Maybe it's all these things. For me, it came to be limestone."

His obsession with limestone was seen by the Keepers of the Recipe and the professors in California as an eccentricity that was likely to cause him rapid and well-deserved insolvency. They all believed—the New World believed—that climate was the key. Soil didn't matter. The sun did.

By European standards, most of California and Australia is too warm for good wine. In the early years, the Californians thought this an advantage; this extra heat would just guarantee a ripe crop every year. The professors at Davis, notably George Selleck's old friend Maynard Amerine, developed a Heat Summation Scale that categorized all regions in the state from One—the coolest—to Five, by measuring their average annual temperatures, and that designated which grapes should be grown in each area. European theories about soil were thrown out the window. If the right grape was planted and European winemaking methods used or improved on, why then, by the use of superior technology the wines should taste even better.

And so they studied every minute aspect of the grape and its juice. They ran it through their laboratory analyses and their centrifuges and their spectrophotometers. They pulled out the malic, tartaric, citric, tannic and phosphoric acids, the proprionic and acetic acids; they made the malic over into lactic and studied that. They watched the long-chain polymers form in their petri dishes. They fermented at low temperatures and high, and then in the middle. They grew yeasts and mutated them. They killed off the wild yeasts and started again. They used glass and stainless steel and oak barrels. They pumped the wine over the cap instead of pushing it down. They filtered and fined, racked and drained. They did everything they could. And though they came up with some dull wines, "white-coat wines" as they were called, they also made some pretty interesting wines. What they didn't get, though, was an interesting pinot noir. The pinot noir continued to elude technological solution—the more sophisticated the technology, the more stubborn pinot noir became. The only thing they never seemed to learn was to leave pinot noir alone.

Jensen, as we shall see, didn't reject technology. But he wanted to use it as an aid to understanding, not as a substitute for it.

To believe that the centrifuge can help you make better pinot noir is like saying a computer can help a lover write better love letters. It can't. Only passion can do that.

But all this really does set the professors' teeth on edge.

There's ample European evidence for the importance of *terroir*, crudely defined as soil, but in reality something closer to the essence of place, which includes the soil, the climate, the aspect, the slope, the way the soil is worked. The wine merchant Kermit Lynch, a romantic about wine and a fulminator against anything but the ancient methods, described in his book *Adventures on the Wine Route* how in some obscure hamlet north of Burgundy he came upon one of his suppliers. "He had three vineyards in three different *terroirs*, limestone, flint and clay, and he bottled them all separately. Here were wines from the same grape, the same cellar, vinification and vintage, but tasting them side by side one encountered three remarkably different personalities." Lynch's view is that the grape is dominant, but not a domestic tyrant; she must be part of a true *ménage à trois*, in love with both soil and climate.

In Josh Jensen's beloved Burgundy, they've no need for laboratory evidence or even for field trials to persuade them of the primacy of soil in this relationship. They had the evidence of their own senses and of hundreds of years of educated drinking planted deep in their psyches. André Noblet would simply pour a glass of his own Romanée-Conti and a glass of La Tâche, a contiguous parcel under the same proprietorship, and rest his case. The soils in those parcels are minutely different. In the labs, they've isolated a mineral in Meursault soil not found in the soil right next door at Puligny. The producers of those two great wines just *know* that the precise mineral composition of the soil is part of what they call the *goût de terroir*, the flavor of the place, and is the reason for the differences, minute but profound, between them.

It's possible for an educated palate, touring the small peasant proprietorships of Burgundy as well as the great *domaines*, to encounter pinot noirs that will taste and smell variously of cassis, cherry mint, blackberry, currant, raspberry, black cherry and herbs of various kinds, and (if really educated) to place them precisely on the bench of the Côte d'Or.

The Burgundians will point out how accurate the ancient classifications of quality still are. Families come and go, they point out, winemaking changes and so do techniques. Fashions dictate changes in style. Why, even the climate changes. Only the *terroir* doesn't change, and the *terroir* dictates the character of the finished wine.

The Californians, for their part, point to the steadying influence of tradition as being at least as important as soil in this long continuity, since the Burgundians (they'll say, with some asperity) are not exactly experimenters at heart. But, the Burgundians reply, the New World cannot be expected to understand, since it's the trial and error of centuries that has established where each grape does best, right down to minute parcels of a particular field on a particular slope. It has worked for centuries. Why change?

The solution to the mystery very likely lies in Lynch's *ménage*, in some combination of factors—the composition of the soil and subsoil, its capacity to hold water and warmth matched against the water and warmth available, the vineyard's slope and elevation. Even then, a great crop will depend on the vigor of the vine, the care and tending it received, its pruning and the number of sunlight hours it received at various stages in the season. From the time the vine buds to the vintage, every drop of rain, every hour of sunshine and degree of heat has its eventual effect on the finished wine. Too little rain in the spring is always a problem. Rain in September dilutes the grapes and creates the risk of mildew. The perfect balance between rain, sun, temperature and humidity has never been determined—the wine gets character from the interaction of them all. Bright sunlight ensures ripening, but overcast skies seem to enrich the grapes with minerals that give the wine long life and complexity.

For the purposes of our bottle of Calera Jensen pinot noir, it's enough to know that Josh Jensen's heart remained on the Côte d'Or. He'd sampled the Rhône, he'd done Bordeaux, he'd visited the Loire and still Burgundy remained his obsession. "Pinot noir and chardonnay were exactly what I myself liked to drink, and I wanted to spend my life making things I'd want myself. This is a very subjective issue."

But he was the son of a dentist, not of a Baron, and he couldn't afford Burgundy itself.

In Burgundy, there was no longer mystery, only money. It was known—exactly—where good wine could be made, exactly where great wine could be made and exactly where greater than great wine could be made. It was also known where those things were permitted to be done by bureaucratic fiat. And the prices of the real estate were exactly co-relative to those qualities—to make great wine would cost half a million dollars per acre.

"These days," says Jensen, "it would be a million, and so with all the money I could scrape together from my family and everything and everyone I knew, I wouldn't have been able to get even an acre of green land in Burgundy, whereas the first property that I bought in San Benito County was three hundred and twenty-four acres, and I got it for eighteen thousand dollars."

In any case, he wanted to go home to California to make his mark; he liked the challenge of trying to do well in a new place, the notion of being a pioneer, with its built-in unknowns and question marks.

❖   ❖   ❖

The first thing he did when he returned to California was to visit the
Bureau of Mines to obtain a set of geologic maps of the state. He was
looking for limestone.

"The whole state has been meticulously mapped geologically. If
you want, say, to find granodiorite rock, you can find it on the maps.
If you want schist, basalt, whatever, you can find it on those maps.
Unfortunately, it turns out the Golden State is pitifully thin in limestone." He looked everywhere, from the Oregon border to Los
Angeles, but there was hardly any limestone to be found. There was
much more in other states—Texas, say, or Alabama—but he wanted
to stay in California. "Partly because I was from here, and partly

because it's a lot easier to do things when you have the structure of
an industry near you. The Oregon industry didn't exist then, only a
few pioneers starting up. And nothing very much in Texas."

He learned just enough geology to be able to tell one rock from
another and to be able to pick out what he wanted—the strata of cal-
careous (limestone-bearing) rock, or carbonine, a more general term
that includes calcium carbonate (limestone itself). He'd also have settled for dolomite, which is half calcium carbonate and half magne-
sium carbonate.

Limestone doesn't always look like chalk, and it's easy to become
confused. There is, however, a simple test, easy to perform—carbonate and dolomite will fizz in contact with hydrochloric acid.

"I had a Volkswagen camper when I came back from Europe, and I'd drive around to these places out in the boondocks. I'm surprised I didn't get shot. I'd drive to the end of these dirt roads, some of them pretty remote and obscure, spend the night, hike around the property, look at it from the road, and then, if it looked plausible, I'd find out if there was limestone there, as the map suggested.

"I had a small eyedropper and a tiny bottle of hydrochloric acid, and I'd dribble a few drops of acid onto the rock. In all that time, I never quite finished one bottle of acid. If it turned out the maps were right—they weren't always—and if the land was not too steep or too low or too high or too hot or too cold or too windy or too this or too that, I'd mark it down as promising. It couldn't be too close to a city, either. I didn't want to spend time and money and be enveloped in ten years by a mushrooming city. I didn't want to develop a world-class vineyard only to have it ripped out and turned into a supermarket.

"Oh, I looked everywhere. I looked at Trinity County, practically at the Oregon border, up in some very high elevations. But it was too cold there, frost too late in the spring and into the summer. There are some nice limestone deposits in Big Sur, overlooking the ocean. But the climate on the Big Sur coast is wild—eighty-mile-an-hour winds, which would thrash the vines and defoliate them."

The land not only had to have limestone. It had to have a climate suitable for grape growing. "The Burgundians taught me that limestone made the best pinot noir. Of course, you can grow pinot noir on other soils. And growing pinot noir on limestone in the middle of a desert is obviously not much use. Although ..."—here he paused, and a thoughtful look came over his face—"it would be challenging to plant some pinot noir on limestone in tough conditions. A desert, though, would be maybe too tough—it's so hot that the grapes would have very little color. Pinot noir tends to lose color at high temperatures. So yes, the other factor was that once I had found some limestone I had to make sure it wasn't too hot, wasn't too cold, and in other ways was suitable."

He'd sift through the temperature and heat-gradient records kept by the state but, with his inborn distrust of bureaucrats everywhere,

he also talked to the farmers surrounding the parcel he was interested in. "If they told me, 'Yeah, I grow peaches here,' well, I knew I
could also grow pinot noir grapes there."

It took him two frustrating years to find the parcel he wanted.
Meanwhile, to support himself, he talked himself into a job as restaurant critic for the *San Francisco Chronicle*. "At that time, in 1972, there
were no restaurant critics working in the city. They took a risk with
me and I did it for two and a half years."

His family, his potential investors, were aghast at this leisurely
search for the perfect limestone vineyard. Other would-be winemakers bought a nice gentle slope somewhere, preferably in Napa or
Sonoma (well, if you must have cool breezes for pinot noir, why not
around the southern end of Napa, in Carneros, close to the Bay?)
and settled down right away to get on with it.

Josh didn't just want to make wine, though, he wanted to make
the best pinot noir in America, and he was stubborn, so he persisted.
He spent fully two years talking to suspicious cattlemen, grumpy
landowners and hostile deer hunters. "Hello Mr. X, you don't know
me but I'm just a young man looking for some property to buy, I
want to plant a vineyard on your hillside, I'm going to grow one of
the great wines of the world right here, yeah sure, you have some
limestone on your property and that's why I'd like to buy this part of
your land."

"Yeah, right," they'd say, and chew a little tobacco, or spit a little,
and then go back to their ranchhouses, shaking their heads.

He had to deal with the inborn conservatism of the ranchers, most
of whom owned huge tracts of land and were hardly interested in
severing small parcels of a hundred acres or so. "Even when I didn't
get a flat-out no, they'd say, 'Well, yeah, maybe, in some years perhaps,' but they were never going to sell, not really."

After two years of searching he came to the Gavilan Mountains.
This was not, traditionally or obviously, grape country. There was
one other winery, Chalone, on the western side of the mountains, facing the ocean. The eastern slopes, where Jensen ended up, were serious back country, less suitable for grapes than for manzanita and

wild oak, for cattle, for hunting, for wild boar and deer and game of all kinds, inaccessible and apparently hostile. Still, high up in the area around Mount Harlan, twenty-two hundred feet above the sea, in virgin scrub, he squeezed his eyedropper and the acid danced and fizzed and sizzled ... bingo!

A three-hundred-and-twenty-four-acre parcel of land close to Mount Harlan mountaintop was for sale. It was owned by a charitable foundation in San Francisco, a trust of the S.H. Cowell Foundation, successor to the Henry Cowell Lime Company, a mining operator. The founder, Henry Cowell, had been the biggest limestone quarrier in the western U.S. at the turn of the century; he had owned limestone deposits all over the west and made cement and other products. The company was left to his son, and his son left it to a charitable foundation. The property had last changed hands in 1903.

This eighteen-thousand-dollar slice of paradise, a precipitous mountaintop made of limestone, containing the ruins of a lime kiln and further ruins of a rock-crushing plant, had a few drawbacks, Jensen admitted. First of all, he didn't have legal access — he'd have to cross someone else's land to get to his, something that offended his libertarian heart. Then, it had no water to speak of, only a creek that ran when it rained, which was when he didn't need a creek. Most of it was too steep to farm anyway, even for vineyards. The power company quoted him outrageous sums to run an electricity line to it, so he would have to do without power. How to pump the non-existent-as-yet water? He'd worry about that later. None of this mattered. It was affordable. He was only thirty years old and he had a whole limestone mountaintop to himself.

The parcel he had to traverse to reach his own was, coincidentally, also three hundred and twenty-four acres. It was owned by a widow, then aged eighty-five.

Jensen asked her if she'd consider selling.

"I don' wanna be a foolin' with it, I jus' don' wanna be a foolin' with it," she said, and dismissed him.

She looked in robust health, good for quite a few years.

He didn't wish her ill. But he was as stubborn as she.

Every year for the next half dozen years, he'd take her flowers and chocolates on her birthday and try to buy it from her, but she "jus' didn' wanna be a foolin' with it."

He became quite fond of her. "You couldn't blame her for not selling," he says now, the grateful proprietor. "When people get old they're afraid they're going to get cheated, made a fool of, and it was just more trouble than it was worth to sell that thing as far as she was concerned."

She died in 1982 at age 93, and her inheritor, her nephew, was happy to sell. For Jensen, it was a prudent buy. The second piece was contiguous to the first, and wrapped around it like a jigsaw piece. It gave him his legal access. It contained even more limestone than his original purchase and had a more secure water supply. It more than quadrupled his supply of plantable acres.

The original three vineyards, the Selleck, the Reed and the Jensen, were all planted on the first parcel, and the newer Mills, chardonnay and viognier vineyards on the second. In 1992 Jensen was eyeing other sites too. Just over the hill is a dolomite quarry and he believes it would be "interesting" to attempt a wine from that soil, since it's analogous to limestone. "In fact, there may be a spot, many spots, around here that would make even better wine than Calera does now. It's hard to believe I picked the perfect spot first try. And here's another challenge: there may be places in other states where there's limestone, where we could make good pinots—Texas, say, or Alabama."

Mount Harlan gave him what he wanted. The heavy limestone deposits crowning the peak ensured that the easily erodable rock traveled downhill, washing into the soil. Better, it was only twenty-five miles from the Pacific and Monterey Bay, and the fog funneled in by coastal valleys all summer creates warm days and cool nights—ideal conditions for pinot noir. The determinant of the climate in California is always the ocean—the closer to the ocean, the cooler the vineyards. This is true even in the Napa Valley, where the coolest area is down along the San Pablo Bay, San Francisco Bay and Carneros. But Jensen usually harvests a full two weeks after Carneros and Sonoma. "The climate is great, not like Burgundy. I've always thought that great wines are produced in Burgundy despite their crappy weather, not because of it. A friend of mine lived in Dijon for exactly a year and says he saw the sun only nine days. Here, we do get fog and the benefits of the marine influence, but we don't get that horrible icy wind that the Salinas Valley gets off Monterey Bay. In fact, the way we keep our winery cool is by fans that come on at night and blow in the cool night air.

"So limestone isn't enough by itself. If that was all there was, you could mix it into your soil and plant wherever you wanted. Mount Harlan gave me the other ingredients too. Still, in my opinion, climate is secondary to soil."

It's one thing to own a mountain of scrub and limestone and have the intention to make a wine to rival the great wines of Vosne-Romanée, but how do you get there from here?

For all the years of his search, Jensen had been keeping mental lists, picking up skills where he could. It was easy to see what was needed. He could tick them off in his head. You need somewhere to live. You need machinery—you're a farmer now. You need to be able to rip out the chapparal brush, which is mostly wild lilac and manzanita, and scrub oaks, root and branch, but mostly root, so you need a deep cultivator. You need a tractor to prepare the land. You need mechanical hoes and mowers. You need power, a generator. You need fences, miles of fencing and thousands of posts, to keep out the deer and the boar. Gates and locks. You need trellis posts and trellis wire, figure the rows about ten feet apart, that's about a mile an acre, figure twenty-four miles of trellis to start. You need water. Your creek runs dry in the critical months, so you need shallow (you hope) wells to start. You need pumps. You need an irrigation system. Drip irrigation along every row to every vine. Another twenty-four miles, of hose this time.

And of course you need vines. What rootstock and what clone to graft? Where do you get 'em? How to be sure of quality?

That's just the vineyard.

You want to make wine in the meantime? To buy grapes from somewhere else for a year or so while your vines mature? You need a winery. Can be just a shed, a warehouse, but then you'll need labor and pumps and ... what else?

For starters, you'll need crushers and destemmers and fermentation tanks, preferably stainless steel and expensive. Another couple hundred feet of food-grade plastic hose. Presses. Storage tanks. Settling and mixing tanks. Barrels—you want to make good wine, you have to buy oak barrels, preferably from France. You can't handle and clean all those yourself—you must have hired hands. You need somewhere to fine the finished wines. You need a bottling plant ... Well, maybe the bottling plant can wait until your wine is readier. Scrap the bottling plant for now. Check into mobile plants like they have elsewhere. Look into bottles, corks. Have to have labels, too—better think about a design. And a name. You'll need an inventory control system of some kind ...

You'll need all of these things before you can make wine. And then you'll have to keep the wine for a year or two before it's ready to sell, so you need warehouse space.

Most of all, what you need is money. Lots and lots of money.

VI

In which hilltop wilderness is
turned into vineyards, and given
suitable names. The first vines are
acquired and planted

The first three hundred and twenty-four acres cost Jensen eighteen thousand dollars and he put that up himself. Then he went looking for money.

The first source was family. "My dad encouraged me to start the winery and invested in the project in the beginning when, I must say with twenty-twenty hindsight, it certainly had to look like a hare-brained scheme, and he remains one of my partners to this day." He formed a partnership with his family—his parents, actually, since brother and sister sensibly declined—and Bill Reed (the only non-family member he's ever taken on as a partner, except for the silent and brooding presence of various banks). Father and mother were, at first, amused by their son's growing obsession, for obsession it was, as Josh now willingly admits. "They were amused and interested at first, and subsequently they were sort of horrified," he says, cheerfully unmoved by any trauma he might have inflicted on them.

Bill (William Garrard) Reed, now with an eponymous Calera vineyard named after him, did have some connection, however distant, with family and Josh always felt they were "almost related." Reed was born in Shelton, Washington, in 1908 and died in Seattle in 1989. His grandfather, Sol Simpson, had been employed by Jensen's mother's family in the northwest lumber business before starting his own small operation, Simpson Timber Company, on a hope and a prayer. His son-in-law, Mark Reed, built the company into a strong regional presence and then Bill, in a spectacular business career that started in 1931, lifted Simpson into the ranks of major American companies. Josh remembers him with great affection. "In 1971 he graciously stepped aside as CEO, even though he really had no desire to retire, when his own son, William Junior, said he was ready to run the company. How many fathers would do that?"

For years Reed Senior wrote the brash young winemaker a stream of unfailingly encouraging letters, always supportive and upbeat, even during the long years when Calera was clearly struggling and a number-crunching capitalist would have recommended liquidation. Josh believes that Reed's decision to invest in Calera at the outset was crucial, as it appeared to validate the project, particularly with his parents. "He even put up with having to go down to the Seattle police station to get fingerprinted, part of the glamour of owning a winery, courtesy of the federal bureaucrats."

In 1981 Josh wanted to increase his personal ownership of Calera and asked Reed if he'd sell his interest. The old man was reluctant because he enjoyed the eccentric investment, but agreed. "We had the shortest, easiest negotiation I'd had in my business career. Bill sold me his interest, and remained a true friend and Calera booster always."

To buy Reed's share, to inject more money into a cash-starved operation and also to have a little something for himself (he was by then raising a family, having married Jeanne a few years earlier), Josh needed a source of cash. His mother's family still controlled a small privately owned lumber company, the primary source of her family's wealth. Josh had inherited a small block of stock in the company and wanted to sell it.

This wasn't so easy. A tiny interest in a privately held lumber company in the northwest? How to value it? How to introduce non-family investors to a family business? "My uncles ... Well, they didn't want to help me in my folly. They kept saying they didn't want me to make a fool of myself. That was understandable. Nor was it a minority opinion at the time. I remember many people telling me I was a fool, that I was going to lose my shirt. I said, unless I sell my stock I won't even have a shirt to lose. Of course, after it became clear I was going to make it, behind my back the same people would say, 'Oh, anybody could have done that, it was so predictable, it was like shooting fish in a barrel.' Though, to give credit where due, there were also people who told me I was going to lose my ass and told my family that, and some of them now come up to me and tell me, 'You remember what I told you? How wrong I was!'"

His uncles delayed and stalled, always ready with a good reason not to let him sell his shares. "Maybe it was the taxes ... Then it was, 'No, we'd like to buy you out but even if we wanted to we couldn't because there's this paragraph, or this subsection, or this technicality ...' They always found reasons why not, never a reason for. It was all baloney. So I set out on a four-year project to try to sell my stock. Eventually I sold it."

His only partner now is his father and it's a partnership only in the winery, not the vineyards. "In the Burgundy model," he says, "which is also my model, the vineyards are everything, the winery nothing. A winery is just a place to store barrels." In this unique case, this is not entirely true: the Calera winery, gaunt and ugly as it is, is more than a warehouse. It's still one of the few (perhaps the only) entirely gravity-operated wineries in the world, and valuable for that. Nevertheless, his heart is up in the hills, where the grapes are, and he owns the vineyards outright. It's the land and the vines he feels most fiercely protective about. All else is replaceable.

"The first thing I did after I bought the land was fence it. I had to, or the deer would have gotten everything. Then I planted my test crops and began to farm. I sort of picked up all the necessary skills along the way, by asking questions and watching."

He was living in a trailer with his wife and two small children.

"Remember, when I bought the place, up where the vineyards are, there was no electricity, no telephone, no paved roads, no anything. It was in the boondocks. There was water, but no pumps. No civilization at all, so I rented a five-acre piece from a rancher at the bottom of the hill, where there was a paved road, electricity and a telephone. The trailer was twelve feet by fifty feet, a mobile home, and *small* ..." The young family lived in it for four and a quarter years before starting to build a house in 1978. They finally moved in 1979. By 1982 Jeanne, who had originally hailed from Cleveland, was becoming fed up with Josh's obsession. It was all very well for him — he spent most of his days riding a tractor in the bush or driving around selling wine, as happy as a pig. She finally left for San Francisco with the children and filed for divorce.

The trailer is still there, occupied by the assistant vineyard manager.

Josh acquired the first vineyard parcel in 1974 and planted the first three vineyards, the Jensen, the Reed and the Selleck, the following year. Three years after that, in 1977, he bought the hundred-acre parcel that now contains the winery, a steep thirty-minute drive closer to Hollister, the nearest town, along Cienega Road. This might seem over-large for a winery, but in ranch country a hundred acres was a small parcel, as small as anyone would sever. A dolomite quarry was his nearest neighbor; the only structures on the hundred acres werethe retaining walls and terraces that formed the skeleton of the stone-crusher that was to become the winery itself. The second vineyard parcel, where the Mills, the chardonnay and the viognier vineyards are now planted, came in 1982.

"It takes about twenty minutes to drive from Hollister to our winery, and about thirty minutes from the winery up to the vineyards. It's quite a steep drive up to the vineyards, another thousand feet up. The Gavilan Mountains start at San Juan Bautista in the north and peter out at the south end around King City, so it's a relatively small mountain range.

"Mount Harlan is a small part of the small chain.

"But it's ours, our own mountain."

❖   ❖   ❖

On March 24, 1974, Josh Jensen took a tractor up the mountainside, cleared the brush from a little more than one acre, and with as many friends as he could round up, he planted five hundred test vines of pinot noir over the next two weeks. He remembers the date so precisely because he had only closed escrow on the property the previous day. "I had the rootings already there from the nursery, and if something had snagged the closing of that escrow it would have been big trouble.

"That test patch of five hundred was just to see if they'd be killed by some killer fungus that nobody had ever heard of before. Or, if it would turn out that it was always minus thirty degrees in the winter but nobody had ever realized it because nobody had ever lived up there. Or maybe there was some secret bug or virus or nematode or some other climatic catastrophe that would render it unsuitable.

"Anyway, they seemed to grow okay, although I couldn't give them enough water—just hand watering from a little jerry-rigged tank on the back of a pickup. So in 1975 we put in the rest of what were to be the original twenty-four acres, and put in the real irrigation system, an above-ground drip system."

Those five hundred vines were to become part of the Jensen vineyard, named after his father. They are now eighteen years old, or "in eighteenth leaf." The rest of the Jensen's nine thousand or so vines were planted the following year. They are in seventeenth leaf. They are where our bottle of wine grew under the California sun.

The summer of 1974 Josh Jensen rode the tractor every day, taking his lunch in the fields, coming home to his trailer sweaty and happy. First the hillsides were plotted and laid out, and the three individual vineyards were laid out around their mountain of limestone. The vineyard boundaries are entirely arbitrary—or at least unrelated to soil analysis or other careful matters—which makes the difference in their wines so interesting. The terrain was so rough there was no choice but to plant a little bit here and a little bit over yonder. It would have been cheaper and far easier to farm on an ongoing basis if he'd been able to plant one continuous carpet of vineyard. Alas, such was not the case. The boundaries were determined in a simple way: Jensen would start the tractor at the creek and work his way uphill until it starting slipping, which marked the boundary of that parcel. The process was repeated on the other side of the creek, which yielded another five acres before the tractor couldn't get any higher.

Then the designated slopes were brushed and the trees stumped. The slash was piled up and burned. The hillside was combed by a giant tractor with three deep shanks three feet apart and as deep as six feet down, first one way across the vineyards, and then a second pass at right angles. This was not to break up any hardpan, for Calera had none—there'd been no soil compaction because no one had worked the land before. What it did was to break up the soil to allow deep penetration by the vine roots, and to comb out any remaining tree roots. It was tricky work—the tractor would pull deep ripping shanks straight up some pretty steep slopes, difficult even for a very large machine, but Josh remembers the work fondly. "I was clearing the trees and the brush and getting it burned and fenced, and for me those are some of my happiest memories, those days when I'd work for three days in a row without talking to anybody, because I'd be living in my camper up in the vineyard, on my mountaintop. I'd be up driving the tractor at seven in the morning and I'd take things like hardboiled eggs into the fields. I was never trained to drive a tractor, do construction work. I just picked it up as I went along. I don't drive tractors any more, and I miss it. It was very satisfying to do a good job at that."

By the late spring of 1975 he had three vineyards. Since his training and inclination were Burgundian, it was natural to harvest each plot separately and treat that batch of grapes as a separate wine, in the Burgundian fashion. He'd seen how identifiably distinct were the pinot noirs made from contiguous parcels in Burgundy, and he was sure the same would happen at Calera. It remained only to come up with a name for each parcel and its wine.

In Burgundy the nomenclature had evolved over centuries. There were village names and commune names and names for individual fields. There were fanciful names such as Bâtard-Montrachet and Les Amoureuses, all of them mossy with age, venerable with tradition and inflexible by bureaucratic edict. Jensen thought briefly about such descriptive site names such as Center Canyon or South Slope, but they seemed banal. Stag's Leap was taken and Boar's Run or Gopher Field didn't seem to lend the right tone. In the end he decided to honor some of the men who had helped and inspired him to start and nurture Calera by naming a vineyard after each.

The first and primary vineyard, and still at fourteen acres the largest, is named for his father Stephen. The second, its five acres at sometimes alarming angles, is called Reed, after his first partner, Bill Reed. The third, another five-acre parcel, was named for George Selleck, who had introduced him to wine in the first place. And the fourth and final parcel, added in 1982, is the twelve-acre Mills vineyard, named for John Everett Mills.

Mills was born in San Francisco in 1912 and died in Hollister in 1985. Jensen met him in the early 1970s when he was still searching for limestone. "I confided that I probably had more money than sense and he instantly replied, 'Great! That's what we need out here!'" Mills's family had moved to the Hollister area shortly after he was born. His mother died when he was thirteen, his father five years later, so at age eighteen he found himself sole support of three younger sisters and a younger brother. He managed somehow. He did hard physical work all his life. At various times he worked in the wheat fields of Canada, in mines in Mexico, at Permanente Cement and at the old W.A. Taylor Winery on Cienega Road, about a mile north of where Calera is now located. For most of his working life he was employed by Archie Hamilton, an eccentric mining entrepreneur. In the 1950s Mills built a series of terraces and retaining walls at Hamilton's Cienega Road property, as the start of a hillside rock-crushing plant, but Hamilton soon changed his mind, abandoning the walls and terraces to the elements and the weeds.

Jensen later wrote, in one of his mailers, that "it was more than twenty years later, in 1977, that an eccentric wine guy named Jensen bought the property with the crazy idea of using those same terraces to make the world's first and only completely gravity-flow winery."

After abandoning the Cienega Road site, Hamilton and Everett built an even more elaborate structure up on his mountaintop limestone deposit, near the top of the Gavilan Mountains. Then Hamilton died suddenly, and it too was abandoned. "I started trying to buy that property in 1972 from Hamilton's widow," Josh recalls, "and that was how I came to meet Everett, who by that time was more or

less retired but was still keeping an eye on things for Mrs. Hamilton. When we were building the winery, Everett would stop by from time to time to keep an eye on us and make sure these city slickers didn't do too many stupid things. In his latter years I guess you could say Everett worked for me.

"He used cusswords prodigiously, in fact, practically as much as I do. I delivered the eulogy at his funeral."

The soil in all four vineyards, while containing the requisite limestone, is generally very poor, thin in nutrients, granular in texture, its problems compounded by a six-year drought. It's deep in places—in spots they've dug down five or eight feet and still found soil—but it's not very fertile. "There's an old saying in Burgundy," Jensen says with philosophical optimism, "that asserts that if the soil in Burgundy weren't the richest in the world it would be the poorest, by which they mean that if you grew potatoes or carrots there, you wouldn't get very many potatoes or carrots. Like Burgundy, our land is worth a million or it's worth nothing."

As his Burgundian perspective suggested, the soil in each parcel contains minute differences, not just in its upper few feet but for the thirty or forty feet that the vine roots reach.

The Selleck has a lot of decomposed granite and there are limestone outcroppings above the vineyard—just like the Côte d'Or. The limestone at the top has eroded and washed downhill, and it has its influence on the soil—Selleck contains more limestone than the others. Its soil is also more granular and lighter in color—brown with a little bit of red. The Reed vineyard has the deepest, darkest soils. Before it was cleared, the Reed slope was a mixed oak and pine forest with a lot of leaf mold, and its soil is blacker, with more clay. Its exposure is northerly and the sun leaves it earlier in the day, so it's always the last of the three vineyards to ripen. The Mills is the most consistent in contour and exposure, a regular field sloping down to the southwest.

Within the other vineyards there are markedly different exposures along the mountain's irregular flank. The Jensen, for instance, is usually harvested over the course of a full month, because its south-facing vines mature much more rapidly than its north-facing ones. For some reason the Jensen outperforms most of the others, and Josh hasn't yet had to reject any wine from it.

Although he has no intentions of doing so, Josh believes he could make at least eight markedly different pinot noirs from the current vineyards.

In 1978 he made seven hundred cases of pinot noir from the young vines in his own vineyards, all in half bottles. It was small, a very modest production. But it was his own, his first vintage. He put a few bottles aside, to build the winery's "library" or archive. Maybe one day he'd give a bottle to André Noblet.

VII

*In which clones are seen to
be important. So is the TLC
given the vines, and the way
they are managed*

$\mathcal{Y}$ou don't just phone up a nursery and say, "Send me over fifteen thousand young pinot noir plants." Not if you're driven by that entrepreneurial single-mindedness that teeters between insistence and obsession. Not if you want to prove the nay-sayers, the doubters and scoffers, wrong, not if you *know* it can be done if you have the right place and the right methods and the right ... raw materials.

To make great wine you also need healthy, vigorous vines. And for the correct vines you need to select the right clone.

Remember that pinot noir had, at last count, more than two hundred, or five hundred, or a thousand, clonal variations, ranging from the heavy-cropping *pinot droit* to the small-berried, tiny-bearing *pinot fin*, the vine of Romanée-Conti, and that it mutates, fades and reconstitutes itself more capriciously than any other of the vinifera varieties; remember that pinot noir is one of thousands of varieties of *vitis vinifera*, all of which are tragically susceptible to the phylloxera louse and for safety's sake must be grafted to American rootstocks to protect them from infection (does the graft interpose a barrier to the free rising of sap? No one knows for sure); remember that there are shy-bearing and prolific clones, upright and spreading clones, large-berried clones and small; remember all this and ... how do you choose?

A clone is a population of plants all of which are the descendants of a single individual and are, therefore, genetically identical. Clones have historically been arrived at through mutation and selection. This is not exactly new—the first clones were propagated well before Roman times, when some neolithic farmer hit on the radical notion of propagating through cuttings instead of cross-fertilization, thereby arriving at the modern vineyard, which consists entirely of sexless— or hermaphrodite—plants.

By historical accident, clonal selection in California was left largely to vine growers and viticulturalists (that is, farmers) and not to winemakers, and has therefore been driven more by the need to improve yields and resist diseases than by a search for anything as elusive as quality. This wouldn't have harmed the industry—after all, disease-free vines benefit everyone—if the winemakers had done their part. But they didn't. In the 1970s and 1980s the winemakers came to rely on technological solutions to enological problems. You have poor grapes and you want fine wines? No problem! Extract the maximum color and tannin by extended maceration! Centrifuge the sucker! Fire it up with off-the-shelf superyeasts!

"I'm not primarily a clone man," Josh Jensen says. "I believe in the primacy of soil. However, having said that, it's important to have a proper clone. It's important that your pinot noir vines are small-clustered, small-berried and low yielding. It's important that you have the real thing and not some mutant, light-skinned, over-producing gamay beaujolais or something similar."

But ... A vine can take seven years to reach full bearing maturity. It can take *years*—up to fifteen years in one notorious case, Jensen's own viognier—for approved imported stock to clear quarantine regulations and actually reach the grower. And humans fade faster than vines do—the average winemaker has only about thirty or forty chances in his lifetime to attempt to make superlative wines. You don't want some grim mutant growing in your vineyard to spoil half a dozen of those chances. You want the right stuff, right off.

Which is why everyone cheerfully believes the rumors that Jensen's pinot noir stock came directly from the Domaine de la Romanée-Conti itself, bypassing Customs, quarantine and the prying eyes of bureaucratic inspectors. Or, if not directly, via Chalone. Or possibly that Chalone got its cuttings from Jensen, who got them, somehow, from the DRC, probably by visiting the place and stuffing his raincoat pockets full of vineyard cuttings, which he propagated on a patch of Chalone vineyard when he got to California. Of course, this could just be a canard made up to spook the bureaucrats, who are (rightly) worried about the importation of noxious pests. Bureaucrats just don't understand the passion—the obsession, the Burgundy obsession—for quality.

I offered to turn my tape recorder off while we discussed this matter of clonal origin. Jensen thought this was a good idea and I did so. In a while, I turned it back on.

"Whether or not our clone comes from Romanée-Conti ...," he was saying, "that in itself wouldn't mean the wines will taste like Romanée-Conti wines. If indeed it were the case, this would merely mean that we've got a true, well-selected pinot noir stock and not a mutant, and that we'd be starting with a good chance instead of with two strikes against us."

So it's fair to say that all of the Selleck, all of the Reed and about two-thirds of the Jensen vineyards are planted with this Romanée-Conti-rumored clone. Unless of course they came from somewhere else, from Chalone maybe, or just from bench grafts from a nursery in St. Helena—off-the-shelf pinot noir, as is the remainder of the Jensen.

Josh did buy some vines from St. Helena. Every year, while he searched for the perfect vineyard, he put in an order. "To really be sure of getting the stuff, you have to order a year in advance. Then I'd cancel at the last moment, because I hadn't found my land yet and so had nowhere to plant them, and re-order again for the next year." Finally, having acquired the land, he bought fifteen thousand plants, at a dollar a grafted rooting and twenty-five cents for the non-grafted rootstocks. "We got them planted, me and my friends, the first year I owned the land. We planted the rootstock, the underground part of the vine, a thing about twelve inches long. This has a few buds on the top and some rootlets on the bottom. You graft the buds onto the top once it's in the ground, after it has grown for a year. We planted in 1975, and grafted the pinot noir buds in 1976. A bud from the fruiting variety or scion, in the case of pinot noir, finger-tip thick, is grafted into the rooting with a single dovetail."

All of Calera's vineyards since the original parcels have, by contrast, been planted on their own roots. This means their roots are pure vinifera. Which means they are completely vulnerable to the phylloxera louse — one hundred percent vulnerable and, once infected, one hundred percent dead. This is high-risk farming. Why does he take the risk?

Phylloxera vastatrix, the louse that nearly destroyed the world's wine industry in the nineteenth century, was first seen in Europe in 1869 and exploded through the wine-growing world with a ferocity and vigor that left no defense. The louse had originally come from North America, whose vines had coexisted with it for millennia and had therefore developed an immunity, and the nick-of-time solution was to graft the chosen clonal cutting onto a root of American origin.

Now phylloxera is back in California. There is some controversy about this. The scientists at Davis are calling it Phylloxera Biotype B, and say it's a new and more virulent mutant. Jensen, no fan of the school or of bureaucrats anywhere, feels that this talk of mutants is an attempt to fudge their own ambivalent role in recent clonal propagation.

"They haven't been reading their mail," he says. "The French have been warning for years that the rootstock they pushed on everyone, AxR-1, was not safe, not sufficiently resistant. But it was a high-yielding rootstock, and winemakers planted it on the university's say-so. Everyone, almost, used AxR-1. Well, the French were right. Many growers planted on this rootstock, and now those vines are dying. And once the louse is in your vineyard, it's over. One vine this year, thirty acres the next, three hundred the year after that ..." There are hundreds of planters in Napa who are faced with the ruinous cost of replacing all their vines. Almost eighty percent of Napa and Sonoma are vulnerable.

So is Calera, but Jensen greets the suggestion with the same philosophical shrug with which he responds to questions about the San Andreas Fault. "Our vineyards are extremely isolated, a hundred miles south of San Francisco, and there are no vineyards nearby. The closest one is a couple of miles away but a thousand feet below us in elevation. Hopefully, if there's any serious spread into our county of phylloxera or Pierce's disease or anything like that, it would take a very long time for the organisms to get up the mountain to our vineyard."

He is, however, being careful. Vehicles that have visited Napa wineries are strongly discouraged from the Calera vineyards, and visitors are taken up in the winery's truck or in Jensen's van, with its Mr. Pinot license plate.

Calera's vineyards, even without phylloxera or Pierce's, took a long time to come up to full bearing. Back-to-back droughts, rabbits, birds, gophers, deer, wild pigs, ground squirrels, mildew, leaf roll, oak-root fungus, leaf hoppers and thrips all took their toll. So have downy mildew, oidium or "powdery mildew," white, black and gray rot, red spiders, grubs of the cochylis and eudemis moths, various sorts of beetles, mites and grubs of all kinds. (Most of these are easily combated by the so-called Bordeaux mixture spray, a mix of copper sulfate and lime, which leaves the vines a garish blue until it washes off, but has the twin virtues of being biodegradable and environmentally benign.)

If, as Josh Jensen believes, it's the vineyard (defined as soil and subsoil, slope, water and drainage, temperatures and sunlight) that imparts character to the wine, if the wine you drink is somehow an expression of the fruit you pick, then the choices made in the vineyard are crucial to the quality of the wine itself. A minimalist approach will only take a winemaker so far. Jensen's friend Jacques Seysses, of the Domaine Dujac in Morey-St.-Denis, Burgundy, may believe that because his vineyards are perfectly sited to grow perfect grapes his job is merely to let nature take its course. He claims to "make wine the lazy way." But the vineyard will only impart character; if handled carelessly a wine of potentially great character will turn mediocre. The winemaker's job is to control for, and be alert to, quality. If the grapes are the horse, the winemaker must act as the jockey. In fact, as Jensen has often observed, Seysses is one of the most meticulous winemakers there is.

California winemakers went through their period of trying to make silken wines from sour grapes. The technocratic manipulation of the wine in the winery eventually ran its course and, led by people like Josh Jensen, there's been a return to low-tech, careful winemaking. An aspect of this more humble attitude is an acknowledgment that the raw material is crucial. Great wine, as they've known in Europe for centuries, is grown in the vineyard.

The vineyard, therefore, is where the next great increases in quality are to be found, the next incremental improvements.

A great crop depends on the health and aggressiveness of the vine, the babysitting it receives, the way it's pruned and the amount of sun it gets at various stages in the season. Grapes will reflect every drop of moisture, every ray of sunlight, every degree of warmth. As Jensen puts it, "From here, smart farm managers, dirt guys, can help us greatly."

Some of the vineyard choices are: where to plant, what rootstocks to plant, what clones to graft, what weight of crop (yield) to aim for, how to lay out the vineyard (how far apart the rows, how far apart the vines?), how to trellis, what pruning technique to use, sunlight, how to manage water (the thorny question of irrigation). And then the questions of sprays, fertilizers, pests and diseases, thinning and selection of the crop, and when to pick.

After that, it's over to the winery.

For the purposes of our bottle, we have the Jensen vineyard, fourteen acres of crumbly limestone soil, on the hump of Mount Harlan, and because of the hump, sloping in four directions at once. Some of its vines are planted with store-bought pinot noir; much of the rest may or may not come from the Domaine de la Romanée-Conti, but its vines resemble very closely those of that eminent *domaine*—producing small bunches with very small berries, yielding a high skin-to-juice ratio. They are growing on St. George rootstock.

The Calera pinot noirs are planted in rows ten feet apart, wide enough for tractors and other equipment to move comfortably, and the plants themselves are six feet apart. This is nothing at all like the vineyards in Burgundy.

Pinot noir vineyards look different wherever they are. On the chilly, chalky soil of sun-starved Champagne, they look maniacally regular. In Burgundy, moist and fecund but shy of sun, the rows are close, the bushes dense and close-cropped. In Australia, where sun is a friend and a threat, the rows are wild and impenetrable. In foggy, windy Carneros, they huddle close. Up in the mountains along Cienega Road, water is the critical resource and the vines, while each is rumpled and untidy, are spaced at intervals so that the roots do not fight for each drop of moisture. The Jensen vineyard has only about seven hundred vines to an acre, less than a quarter of the European norm.

They are pruned and trained to a modified cordon system on a three-wire trellis. At the end of each annual cycle, when the grapes have been picked and the vines have gone dormant, they are cut back to two three-foot-long "cordons," which are trained horizontally along the lowest of the three wires. A selected number of buds, usually twelve, is left on each cordon. When the shoots grow in the spring, they are trained upwards and tied to the two upper wires, giving the right balance of leaf to fruit.

There are many other methods of pruning: the espalier and "goblet" systems are the most common. Others are cane-pruning, fan-pruning, low-bush training and high trellising, with many variations on each.

The Jensen vineyard is managed by Jim Ryan and Jensen, asked about pruning, refers questions to him. "In fact, Frédéric [Magnien] can probably give you a better idea of the differences between us and Burgundy. It's always been the area of the business that I know the least about. In the early years I was the vineyard manager, and it's one reason why the vines got off to a bad start. I'm just not a farmer."

The idea behind pruning, which is essentially a kind of "vegetable editing" in Hugh Johnson's phrase, is to control yield—either to maximize yield and ripeness, as in Germany, or in more torrid climates like Spain, to restrict them. The more arid the area, the wider apart the vines and the more floppy the canopy of foliage to protect the berries from the sun. In wetter regions you plant close to prevent each vine being drowned with too much water.

In the Jensen vineyard "canopy management" is an ongoing experiment. This means picking selected leaves off in the growing season from the canes and around the berry clusters. Jensen believes it improves the wine. "I think it accelerates ripening, gives better acid, lowers pH and cuts down on mildew. It also increases the phenolics — the complexity of flavor and the volatile aromas. It adds color too."

It also has another advantage. At the base of each shoot is a bud, and the amount of sun each bud receives governs its fruitfulness the following year. Selected leaf thinning can thus have a considerable effect on the crop the following year. A heavy canopy of leaves will make the vine throw out more foliage and less fruit. Hence the trellising method pulls the fruiting canes upwards, which pulls the leaves away from the fruit, exposing the berries to the sun.

In parts of France, particularly Bordeaux, pruning is entrusted only to experienced people intimate with the vineyard, the vine and the *terroir*. In Australia, where they haven't quite gotten over their technophilia, they are experimenting with a pruning method that more nearly resembles hedgerow management—simply cutting everything with circular saws into a neat hedge. They claim it works just as well. At Calera all pruning is done by hand by the permanent vineyard crew and whatever part-time help is available. It can take several months to complete.

The first decision a winemaker must take after planting and layout decisions are complete is the thorny question of yield. In France, it's axiomatic that low yields intensify flavors. A smaller crop gives you a darker, richer wine that's more flavorful and intense; the bunches sit apart on the vine and they don't rot as easily. The fruit can be left on the vine longer without risk and the grapes mature better. Of course, in Burgundy, which is at the northern end of acceptability for red grapes, low yields have another advantage, which has surely colored its codification of low yields into ironclad edicts (high yields automatically "declassify" the wine from that vintage, degrading a Vosne-Romanée, for instance, to a mere bourgogne): a small crop will also ripen faster.

Bearing a heavy crop is as stressful to a vine as pregnancy is to a woman. But what is "heavy"? What is "high yield"? In California, with its abundant sunshine, bigger crops can ripen well and the Burgundian axiom might be false. Still, it's fair to say that most quality producers believe in low yields.

It's also fair to say that grape growers don't.

Nor, indeed, do the winemakers' bankers, who regard yield as just another name for productivity, and bankers *love* productivity, because it improves the cash flow (in the short term) and pays down those inevitable loans more quickly. (For the same reason, those few bankers who know wine are suspicious of pinot noir—fickleness is not a bankerly approved quality. They don't like its changeableness, nor the time it takes to store it before getting it to market. Which is exactly why they *do* like the exotic viognier, a wine that demands to be bottled fast and drunk the same year—the perfect cash-flow wine, a wine for the accountants.)

At Calera "yield" has another set of referents altogether. The yields have been absurdly low by the already low standards of Burgundy and other high-end producers. That these low yields produced superlative wines is a cause-effect calculation that yet has to be finally resolved.

Calera's low yields were caused by drought, lack of natural water, bureaucratic harassment, lack of nutrients in that limestone soil, pests, stress and inadvertence. And probably by bad (or good, depending on your perspective) karma too.

In Burgundy, the "magic number" for a yield is forty-five hectoliters per hectare, above which most *premiers crus* require declassification. However, yields can vary for "good" wines (as opposed to "great" wines) anywhere from fifty to one hundred hectoliters per hectare, with enormous—and adverse—effects on quality. In the more fertile fields of California, and under the western sun, it's quite common for table-grape growers to attain yields of ten to fifteen tons of grapes per acre, or one hundred and fifty to two hundred and twenty-five hectoliters per hectare, a sure recipe for mediocrity. With healthy vines, four tons per acre can yield first-class wines, though some producers say anything over three won't do.

At Calera, three tons would be a miracle.

In 1988, the second year of the most recent drought, the yield was a pitiful half ton per acre. In 1989, 1990 and 1991, Calera struggled to get a mere one ton per acre. Which is why the '92 vintage, achieved with "average" rainfall rather than the meager water of previous years, was so extravagant by Calera standards.

"Mind you, we also gave our vines their first real fertilization in '91 and '92, and that, combined with additional water, significantly improved our yields. It proved our land needed nutrients as well as water. The 1992 rainfall was just average and we got terrific yields, for us, a record in five of our six vineyards: two tons per acre on the Jensen, Selleck and Reed, two and a quarter on the Mills, three and a half in the chardonnay, and four in the viognier. Only the Jensen ever had a better year, and that was in 1987, when we got two thousand one hundred and seventy-eight cases from it—this year we'll get nineteen hundred."

The 1990 Jensen, the vintage I would follow through the system, was from a more typical Calera yield: nine hundred and seventy-five cases of wine were made from the fourteen acres, a driving-bankers-to-distraction yield of about one ton an acre.

For the '86 and '87 vintages of the Mills pinot noir, and the '86 through '89 Mount Harlan chardonnays, the wines carried another line on their bottle labels: Young Vines. These vineyards were planted in 1984 and finally dropped the designation in 1990, the vintage year of our bottle of Jensen.

Grape growers date vines by "leaf," that is, by growing season. Vines, whether planted in February or July, are equally considered to be "first leaf" that year. First leaf just means they're in their first growing season. Third leaf—that is, the third growing season—is the earliest a vine can yield a crop. Wines from young vines usually have less concentration, less stuffing, less color and less body.

The converse is also true — the older they get, the more concentrated the finished wine. On the other hand, yields drop. You get fewer and fewer grapes and the wine becomes greater and greater. Jensen gets positively dreamy contemplating venerable vines. "Wines made from the very oldest vines, wine from vines, say, a hundred and twenty years old, would be sublime, but you'd only get a few bottles per row. So in order to make a business of it you have to replant portions periodically. The standard commercial practice is to pull the vineyards out at about age forty. I'm a contrarian and I'd be inclined not to do that, but I'll be pushing up daisies by the time that decision has to be made." The Jensen vines from which our bottle was made were planted in 1974 and 1975, and were in fifteenth leaf at vintage time. "So forty is still a way off. It won't be up to me. I like old vines, but my children or someone else might want to take them out."

VIII

*In which the drought takes its toll,
and a vendetta is conducted
against our winemaker in the
matter of water. Enter the Enemy*

*I*t doesn't rain enough in California, even when there's no drought. And when it does rain, it rains at the wrong times, in winter. So grape growers must perforce irrigate.

This drives the French to distraction. They're convinced that irrigation spoils the grapes—that it cannot possibly have the same beneficial effects as natural rainfall. They've even made irrigating vineyards illegal. Of course, that's all very well for them to say—most years they get far more rain than they need and drainage is more important than moisture retention in French soil. Which is why the Burgundy sites that produce the best wines are almost always on well-drained slopes. (On the other hand, the French will readily toss bags of sugar into their fermenting wines to counteract over-acidity caused by meager sunshine. This "chaptalization" is illegal in California. In truth, even the French think there's something faintly disreputable about it and hardly discuss it in polite company. To each his own adulteration.)

Most new grape growers in California install drip irrigation systems, and this is a source of further contention. Obviously vines must have water, since overstressed plants won't produce a decent crop, but the French view is that if you deny a vine easy access to water you'll force it to root deep—thirty feet or more—and it will pick up interesting and flavorful minerals along the way. Irrigation, especially the kind of precisely controlled system practiced at Calera, causes the roots to bunch near the surface, in the moist cone caused by the drip. A vine dependent on this shallow water won't need to go deep and it will lose access to all those interesting minerals.

Josh Jensen hardly enters this debate—without irrigation, his vines would die. He must irrigate or perish.

He does this in a simple way. A subterranean hose system leads from the water source—more on this in a moment—to the head of each row, where it then enters a smaller rubber hose three-quarters of an inch in diameter. This hose is tied to the same wire as the vine's cordon, the lowest of the three trellis wires. There's one emitter per vine, and the emissions are controlled by head valves, which deposit about a gallon an hour, exactly where the roots of the vine await. The system is very sparing of water.

Assuming there's enough reservoir water in the first place, drip irrigation has another advantage. Water stress, which is viticultural jargon for drought, can be precisely controlled and a nervy grower can even attempt what the academics are calling "deficit water management"—that is, rationing water at critical moments. Water is most essential at two points in the growth cycle—when the berries set after flowering and when they turn color; vines *must* have water at those times. Most growers who irrigate cut back after the grapes color. At this point grapes simply store excess water, diluting the skin-to-juice ratio so essential to great wine. On the other hand, if the weather is very hot, the grapes' ripening system will shut down for self-preservation, and the vine must be watered to keep it cool. Deliberately rationing water before *véraison* (coloring) will therefore slow the grapes' growth, and rationing it afterwards may, if one is extremely careful, encourage ripening without increasing cluster weight. By bungling the rationing you could also, of course, simply kill the bunches. It's high-risk management.

Josh Jensen uses his system for another purpose. It's the most efficient way of delivering liquid nutrients like nitrogen to the root system.

For the Jensen vineyards, and for our bottle of wine, then, it's not so much a question of whether to irrigate but whether there'll be enough water to do it properly. Water is the biggest problem Calera faces. The merits of Josh Jensen's long fight with a multiplicity of enemies is not our concern, but it isn't surprising that he feels beleaguered, because those enemies range from the natural forces of a six-year drought to a politically correct appreciation for mystical Indian custom and ceremony. In this volatile mix can be found an elderly Judas (Jensen's phrase), the "eco-terrorist stormtroopers" of the California department of Fish and Game and a secretive mining company that Jensen believes is slowly buying up land around him, with the intention of turning his precious mountain of limestone into cement and miscellaneous rubble. There's even a Hong Kong gambling syndicate in there somewhere.

Of course all farmers complain about the weather. I learned this when I was just a kid and watched the worry about water consume my grandfather's life. He'd stand for weeks on the earthen levee of his only reservoir, watching the levels drop, until the mud on the dam floor cracked in the heat. Then his market garden crops died and his animals starved. Every few years or so, though, he'd watch as the rains came in torrents and the dam overflowed, and the mud walls were swept away in flash flooding, waves of muddy brown water washing away the dreams of another year.

In any case, even in more benign climes than southern Africa it's a rural cliché that the current year's weather is always the worst. In Calera's case, this cliché has come to have considerable validity. If you ask Jensen about water, his face will turn grim. He will also talk without interruption for an hour, never repeating himself.

"Generally, the story of our vineyards is one of not enough water. It's a real limiting thing for us. The only exceptions were a few years after I bought the second property, in 1982. Now, in 1992, it's worse than it's ever been. We've had five years of drought and one year of normal rainfall. Last year was fairly normal, but not enough rain fell to replenish the water supply, fill the reservoirs or affect the water table.

"There are two small creeks that used to run through our vineyards, but there hasn't been surface water in them for all of those six years.

"The source of our water in the first years were two shallow wells we dug with a bucket rig alongside one of our creeks, but they never produced much water. We planted most of our vineyards in '75 and went immediately into the '76-'77 drought, the worst in California for years until the present one. So for the second and third years our vines were in the ground we had back-to-back droughts, and there was not enough water to take proper care of them.

"The first year, when we only had five hundred vines, I watered them by hand. The following year we put in our drip system, the source for which was those two little shallow wells. Our water tanks were two backyard swimming pools, the above-ground kind, about twenty feet across. I think they held about twelve thousand gallons each. In hindsight I realize it was a false economy, but we didn't have a lot of money then. That was a cheap way to get a tank.

"We placed one of the 'tanks' down the canyon from the two wells and used a gravity siphon to shift the water. From there, we used a fifty-gallon-a-minute pump to move it into the second tank a couple of hundred feet up. That second one was higher than any of the vines and we could use gravity to irrigate the whole vineyard.

"What we should've done was spend another fifteen or twenty thousand dollars to put in some sizable storage tanks, twenty thousand or thirty thousand gallons, and store up more water each time, giving the vines all the water they wanted. The wells would have filled those tanks, at least that first year.

"A reservoir already existed on the second property when I bought it, dating back to the thirties. In 1982 we built three more small ones.

"There was no shortage of water then. In '82 and '83 we were afraid the rain was going to wash out all four of our reservoirs. In '84, '85 and '86 there was plenty of rain and water flowed down Harlan Creek as late as July 1. When we do get good rains we get a triple benefit—the vines get "natural" irrigation, the ponds fill up and wells improve too.

"In May and June we'd irrigate our vineyards. During those wet years, we'd use less water. Jim would irrigate one day and take the dam down half a foot, the next morning it would be up flowing over the spillway. You didn't see much visible surface water, but there'd be springs replenishing it.

"In '87 there was virtually no rain. What we did get soaked in gently. At the end of the previous season we'd pulled the pond down to two-thirds or half full. Then, in the winter, it didn't rain at all. The '87 season was itself a dry year and we said to ourselves, 'It's a good thing we've got the water.' So we pumped it all on the vines and we got the biggest crop we'd ever had, forty-three hundred cases.

"But that winter was worse. We had emptied the pond by September of '87 and nothing went into it in '88—you could walk across the bottom in your best shoes—across all four of the reservoirs. We had a seventy-five percent decline in our crop in 1978. We really got clobbered.

"On the advice of an old coot hereabouts, we dug a little box lined with redwood planks in Harlan Creek on the newer property, locating it higher than our reservoir and we got what looked like a bonanza—twenty gallons a minute out of an eight-foot-deep box. Still, by June and July of '88 our vines were looking like they were going to die. We had tiny amounts of water—five gallons per minute in August—and we had to husband it until the end of summer, and the two original shallow wells were dry as a bone because the water table was down.

"By the end of the '88 year, we were down to five and then three gallons a minute. That kept forty-four acres of vineyard alive. Three gallons a minute around the clock comes to a surprising amount of water, but it was still like going around with an eyedropper. We had only thirteen hundred cases of wine that year. Very intense, over-concentrated wine, tasted more like late harvest zinfandels than pinot noirs. It was pretty scary."

We were sitting in a restaurant in the little village of Tres Pinos, near Cienega Road, demolishing steak-and-salad and a bottle of

Calera's Central Coast pinot noir. There was a noisy party of locals in the corner, but Jensen's anger easily carried to the tape recorder, balanced, ironically, against a water jar at the corner of the table. He thumped the table, making the cutlery dance, spilling a few drops of water. He didn't notice.

"You've got to understand," he said, leaning forward and waving his knife. "For the six years of this drought our ponds have been dry. But it wasn't just us. Remember, this drought affected not just the Gavilan Mountains. It was true of L.A., Idaho, Utah, most places in the western U.S.

"Most of these places had the sense to admit there was nothing they could do about it—you can't just make it rain whenever you want. Our neighbors downstream are the only ones in all the west to know exactly what causes their water shortage—it's that SOB up on the hill, Josh Jensen.

"They didn't think their low water had anything to do with years and years of drought, oh no. They didn't accept that if a waterfall dried up it might have something to do with the fact that it hadn't rained for seven years. Oh no, no, no. They didn't understand that ground water, particularly, is like a bank account: you can't draw out more than there is. They blamed me, and they didn't want me to be able to store any water at all because of that. They filed protests. Our opposition was figureheaded by Ann-Marie Sayers, a half-Indian woman who said we had dried up the waterfall she wanted to use for Indian ritual purposes. She claimed she wanted to develop her property as a 'heritage area' and was going to build an earth lodge and a sweat lodge to accommodate these ceremonies. The real Svengali was this old coot I mentioned, he was eighty-two years old, Howard Harris, who, it turns out, was actually the agent of the Graniterock Corp., a secretive mining concern from Watsonville. There's a lot of granite on the mountain, and limestone, and essentially they want my mountain for mining purposes. They've already got four different parcels under Harris's name and Harris has admitted in depositions that he's just their 'nominee.' They have acquired a piece of government land, a piece from a group of Hollister real-estate speculators and they bought one other piece, and Sayers has sold half her land and all her mineral rights.

"What they're trying to do is put a collar around me. If they buy two more pieces of land they'll have me surrounded. There's one parcel downstream from Sayers that's owned by a Hong Kong gambling syndicate, believe it or not, and they've been trying to buy it, and if they get that I'm cooked. They'll have me isolated on that side and then they can try to force me out by using legal challenges and hassles to hamstring my rights to the creek and my water." (It's fair to say at this point that Graniterock Corp. president Steve Woolpert has been quoted as saying, "Jensen has a vivid imagination.")

"In November 1990 the State Water Board bureaucrats investigated. They found a couple of technicalities, but essentially said we were using water efficiently and that the water we used wouldn't have gotten down the canyon anyway, it would have disappeared through what they called 'evapotransporation.'

"This didn't satisfy our neighbors. They kept at us, and in July 1991 there was a second report, which was a real chamber of horrors. This report simply accepted every argument our opponents made, no matter how spurious, and rejected every argument we made. It rejected all our operating assumptions and essentially said we didn't have the right to take or store water."

Nevertheless, water is subject to tripartite jurisdictions in California, and there were some sources the bureaucrats couldn't touch. The most secure source is ground water, because landowners have the absolute right to take that, so Jensen concluded that he'd have to drill several new deep wells. He did so in the spring and summer of 1992.

"We were real careful where we drilled them, too. We were determined not to get caught in the regulatory snare and to anticipate whatever objections they might dream up. For instance, the wells were at least a hundred feet from the nearest creek bed, we encased the top hundred feet with a concrete hermetic seal, we did everything we could ...

"Those wells went down nine hundred feet and a thousand feet, and cost fifty thousand dollars each.

"Then you add the pumps, wires and pipe for another twelve thousand dollars a pop, and we spent a hundred and twenty-four thousand dollars on those two wells.

"Each well is rated at fifteen gallons per minute, which doesn't sound like a lot but when you do that twenty-four hours a day for seven days for twelve months that's almost sixteen million gallons, and that's a lot of water, particularly when you have, as we do, an efficient drip-irrigation system. Eventually we'll store it in a large sealed steel tank, so we won't lose a drop.

"We have no electricity up there, so we will also need a generator some day. This will cost maybe twenty-three thousand to buy."

I started to add the numbers in my mind. The costs were incredible.

"Surely," I said, "if you told a grape farmer down in the valley that you have to use diesel fuel to pump water a thousand feet and only get fifteen gallons a minute, and this from wells that cost more than a hundred thousand dollars, he'd have you committed?"

"Yeah, sure," he said. "But given the rarefied pricing of our wines and the high economic value of our grapes, it's acceptable for us. Just."

"Was that the end of it?"

"Not at all. We had to hire a geo-hydrological consultant to tell us where to drill the wells, and he cost fifty-five thousand."

"Seems a bit steep?"

"Yeah, well, what're you gonna do? Our legal bills are fifty thousand and running. We had to hire a water engineer. He cost thirty-five thousand. Eventually, to fight off the endless numbers of bureaucrats and to get the endless numbers of permits we needed, we had to hire our own biologist to prove we didn't destroy habitats, our own archaeologist to prove we weren't desecrating a sacred Indian site, our own soils engineer to make sure the compacting of soil was adequate, and on and on ... It was insane."

Since 1983 Jensen had had four small reservoirs in or near Calera's vineyards, and permits allowed him to store 22.4 acre feet of water. These permits, too, were being attacked, and in an effort not to be stripped of those, he finally stopped representing himself and hired a top water lawyer. On May 27, 1992, they met, with

witnesses, opponents and all, and got an agreement—sort of.
Jensen offered to knock down one dam entirely, leaving only
three. He agreed to give up almost all rights to store creek water.
He agreed to rebuild the remaining dams with an outlet pipe in the
bottom and a constant flow meter and stage recorder in each one,
expensive and costly machinery he'd have to pay for. He agreed
he'd only add water to the reservoirs, up to the permitted level,
from November to March, and only then if there were visible surface water flowing all the way across Sayers's place downstream.

"In any of the six previous years, under this agreement, we'd not
have been able to store one drop of water."

Jensen's water engineer thought he was mad to agree to this kind
of expense for water he might never get. So he shifted ground.

"Instead, we agreed to knock down all but one dam, the largest.
We'd increase its capacity to about ten acre feet from its present
eight. Of course, they barely noticed that we were giving up half our
storage rights—our permit allowed 22.4 acre feet—and demanded all
kinds of permits and permissions for increasing this dam, and
stopped work so often through spurious claims that our contractor
had to take his machinery away several times. The contractor's bill
was for over a hundred thousand dollars.

"Our total water bill *this year* is over three hundred thousand so
far, and they're still fighting us."

Someone once asked Jensen, in the middle of the last drought,
what he'd do if he never received the water he desperately needed.
"I'll do myself in by drinking a glass of cabernet sauvignon," he said
laughing.

He's not laughing about it now. He's feeling strangled.

This story of acrimony and contention, this anxious wresting of water
from parched ground and permissions from desiccated government
procedures, is all part of the particular history of our bottle of Calera
Jensen pinot noir. I drank a glass or two of it that night, but of course
tasted none of the bitterness and anger of the fight to keep it alive,
none of the worry. I suppose the same would have been true years

before, when as a child I ate a bowl of my grandfather's strawberries, produced at such cost and such anguish and such stress, after a year of savage dust storms in the interior of Africa. Then, I tasted only the fruit, and the warmth of the sun. Now, I went back to my room in San Juan Bautista and ate a piece of dried beef with my Jensen pinot noir. It seemed to me the wine tasted faintly, faintly, of violets.

IX

*In which the grapes that will
make our bottle of wine are
beginning to ripen, sweeten and
swell under the California sun*

*I*n March 1989, the shoots that would eventually make the 1990 wines started to swell, small round green buds like little lymph nodes, just below where the current year's leaves and flowers were sprouting. By summer, when the canopy was in full leaf, the small nodes were mostly hidden by the foliage. They remained there all season, not swelling any further, soaking up what sun the leaves allowed. The crop that year was small, pitifully small; the bunches of grapes were tight set, the berries smaller than usual, widely spaced on the canes. The vines were suffering from severe water deprivation; it was the worst year of the drought and Calera was not prepared—its creeks and reservoirs dry, it was subsisting on minuscule amounts of water from the small hole dug in the creek bed, no more than three gallons a minute to water forty-eight acres of vineyards. There was a seventy-five percent drop-off in the crop. The nodes that were to make our wine did nothing. They simply waited their turn, the following year.

The harvest in September 1989 was subdued. Jesus Zendejas hired fewer pickers than he normally would—there just weren't enough grapes to make a full crew worthwhile.

The nodes were left on the canes after the pickers went through.

Then, in the pruning, most of them got cut off. That was quite normal.

The harvest is the death and life of a cycle in the vineyard and in the winery. The grapes have gone to the crushers and the vines look forlorn, empty; they are still in leaf but the fruit has gone. If there's any down time in the vineyards, it will be in November and December. When he was younger and not responsible for a crew, vineyard manager Jim Ryan used to wish for a soaking wet November. "There'd be no reason to go to work, because you just couldn't get there." He laughs. Life is more complicated now. Those of his crew being paid by the hour hate rain; the enforced idleness means they don't get paid. Rain means chores that don't get done. On the other hand ... rain means the reservoirs, bone-dry from years of debilitating drought, would begin to fill. Perhaps even the creeks would run again.

But after the harvest the fall of 1989 was, once again, dry. So he organized his crew for what he calls "slack time, but not down time." His reduced crew had been working literally seven-day weeks for five or six weeks or more, and they needed to catch their breaths. Some of them he let go fishing. "Take a couple of days in November as 'summer holidays.' Then they get Christmas and Easter vacations—that's also time to relax, take trips—because they don't get to take trips in summer."

It wasn't as if there was nothing to be done. In the second week of November there was an infestation of gophers and Ryan assigned a man to set traps. Gophering is a full-time occupation on Mount Harlan; the brazen pests never seem to have down time themselves and they're a menace to a well-run vineyard. His crewman would spend a week setting and emptying the traps. And while he was there, he dealt with other rodents, with rabbits, ground squirrels, rats ... all the many creatures that would feast on young vine shoots in the spring.

There were also a few holes in the fences. Deer, constantly pushing, had broken through in spots. They're a problem in the spring, when they damage the fresh foliage, and they have to be kept out.

Some of Calera's fences are in the bush where they are hard to find and hard to maintain, and constant patrols are necessary.

There's machinery to be serviced in preparation for the next year. There are tractors, sprayers, dusters, disks, harrows, pumps—a number of different pumps of varying capacity to be checked and stored. There's never quite enough machinery—farm managers regard agricultural-implement showrooms the way a computer hacker does a new-products expo; there's always some marvelous new and very expensive toy that, if only we had it, would make our lives that much easier and us more productive. (The seductive part of all this is that it's true, if hardly cost-effective.) Well, so there's maybe not enough machinery, but there's plenty enough to need maintenance. The equipment has to be put away for the winter, greased and stored. Pumps have to be winterized. There are always construction projects on a farm. Maybe build a new tool shed, another barn, a pump house ...

That year, Ryan's crew took down the pumps and irrigation system early. There was no water, in any case, and they might as well do the maintenance while they had time. They tore down all the main junctions and connectors, dismantled all the pumps, checked the main irrigation lines and checked the forty-five miles of hose with their thirty-three thousand drip-emitters to see that they were performing adequately.

Water supply permitting, Ryan likes to water the plants, and give them a shot of nitrogen fertilizer through the drip system, between harvest and dormancy. "That way you know the plant is ready to go, not all stressed out from carrying a big crop. It picks it back up and gets it ready for the spring." The roots keep growing all season, while the vines are holding a crop or putting on new leaves. "Then, well, you've got your crop in and you put the vines to sleep. You know when the vine goes dormant and you get ready for pruning. I usually let the vines go for almost a month before I start pruning. I don't start until the beginning of January."

Ryan's crew doesn't work in the winery and the cellarmen hardly ever visit the vineyards. Jensen tried mixing crews once, getting the vineyard men to come down off the mountain to help when the grapes were in, but it didn't work. The crews resisted each other, there were turf problems, personality clashes. The vineyard workers are, in his words, "sort of ornery mountain men," and they prefer the freedom of working out in the fields. "Not every operation is run that way, but ours is because there's so much physical distance between the two. The vineyard guys grow the grapes and get them to the winery, and that's it."

In 1990, the year of our bottle, pruning started two days after New Year's Day. Pruning must be completed before the first buds swell, which will be sometime in March, and generally the crews aim to finish by the end of February, or mid-March at the latest. Four men moved into the vineyards with their clippers, but after a few days two more were diverted from pruning to gopher-trapping, and Jesus put out the call for more workers. Before the end of the month, because they were falling behind, six men were working the vines. Each man pruned a couple of rows a day and by the time it was done, each had pruned well over seven thousand vines, squeezing his clippers maybe forty-eight or fifty thousand times, possibly more. The long canes were cut off and dropped in the ten feet between rows, to be picked up later, chopped and added as mulch.

Calera vines are trained to a three-wire trellis. In the winter each is cut back severely. Only the trunk and the two cordons spreading three feet on each side (almost touching the next vine, some six feet away) are left permanently. These bilateral cordons are attached to the bottom wire. On each cordon the pruners leave six spurs, growth from the previous season. Six spurs on each side, each spur cut back to two buds, twenty-four buds per vine. The shoots from those buds will grow up towards the sun; they'll either catch the wire above, or the crew will tie them up later.

Pruners have some discretion here. If the wood from the previous year looks particularly healthy, the pruner may leave an extra ten or twelve buds on extra spurs from the cordons. This will add considerably to the eventual crop. A spur the size of an ordinary pencil is the smallest that will carry two buds. Anything smaller is generally cut to one. Anything larger ... As long as the spur looks healthy, if it's round, with clean, fat buds and a little thicker, the pruner will leave a few extra buds. It takes experience and a good eye.

In the early weeks of 1990, the buds looked healthy, normal. The stress on the vines hadn't made for weedy spurs. But there were no extras either—1990 would not be a massive crop.

By March 13, the pruning was done.

One of the men was sent through the vineyards with a mower, to chop the prunings and the weeds so the disks and the harrows and the hoes could get through. That year, because they were a little late, Ryan had the worker make two passes, because the grasses were coming up at that time too.

Then the soil was turned with a disk and after that the hoes went through, one of the men spraying under the vines for weed control.

Ryan also did his first dusting with sulfur in late March. He dusts three or four times a year, to control mildew. "That's the only thing I treat for right now. Some years you get one problem, another year another problem. Our main problem is mildew. In Salinas valley they've got mildew, fungus, bugs, everything. Of course, they spray-irrigate, which leaves water on the vines and the clusters, a perfect environment for bacteria and viruses that grow on vines. So every time they water they have to go back and spray to prevent mildew and bunch rot. Drip irrigation just doesn't cause as many problems. And down in the valley, near Monterey, if one farmer gets a pest the whole damn place will get it soon enough, they're that close together. That's one of the good things about our vineyards, their isolation."

Ryan waited a few more weeks, until the vines had about six inches of new growth but well before berries were forming, and then went through the vineyards and sprayed with a product called Bayleton, a fungicide for mildew. Organic growers won't use Bayleton because it's systemic; unlike a dusting sulfur, it won't wash off. Ryan likes Bayleton precisely because it will stay with the plant through the rainy reason. Then, after the buds have set, he'll begin a dust program, using a tractor-mounted fan. This disappears fast, so there's no danger of fungicides remaining on the fruit in the run-up to vintage time.

The few weeks between the swelling of the buds, in March and April, and the close of the "rainy season" (if there is one that year), about the first of May, is the time in the cycle when the crop is most vulnerable to frost. This is perhaps the single most anxious period in a grape-grower's year. The only moment in the winery that could compare with the fear of frost is the fear of a stuck fermentation — that moment when the fermentation, for no apparent reason, simply stops, leaving the winemaker with a large tank full of sugary, half-fermented muck.

The sweet green growth of April is particularly vulnerable to frost. I've heard hard-bitten vineyard men, many of them as "ornery" as Josh Jensen's mountain men, wax lyrical about these tender green shoots; they become as protective, as solicitous, as worried as the father of a young girl on her first date, and if the date goes wrong, if the abusive hand of Biker Frost damages the young thing, they react with the same pathetic mixture of useless anger and violently protective concern. The worst time of all is when the vine is just about ready to set fruit — the cold will hit the young clusters hard.

The Calera vineyards have not — yet — had a killer frost, and although the elevation protects him to some degree, Jensen is realist enough to know he's going to get one soon enough. There have been serious frosts in parts of California as late as June 1. If Calera does get hit, Jensen has no defense.

"Our specific site up there doesn't have much frost, knock on wood. When I put in those first five hundred vines in 1974, that was one of the things I wanted to know. I needed to know if they were going to be destroyed by rogue frosts. Well, nothing happened.

"If it had, I couldn't have done anything about it. I still can't. We don't have frost protection technology. We'd be dead ducks."

There are two main ways of defending vineyards against frost. Smudge pots — smoky fires that warm the air a degree or two — are used mostly in Europe. The main technology in California is, somewhat surprisingly, to spray water on the vines. It's the same treatment Florida citrus growers use.

The physical principle is simple enough — ice won't drop below thirty-two degrees Fahrenheit, zero degrees centigrade, if there's unfrozen water on the surface. So those growers with spray-irrigation systems (and lots of water) turn on their sprinklers when the alarms go off, usually at about 4 a.m., and the sprinklers go on spraying water until the danger is over. The grower ends up with icicles on his vines, but so long as the pump doesn't give out or the water doesn't run out, the tender green shoots won't be damaged.

The protective window is very small—the shoots are safe to twenty-nine degrees Fahrenheit and the ice won't drop below thirty-two—but it's enough, all the vines need.

However, Calera has neither overhead sprinklers, nor the right pumps, nor anywhere near the amount of water needed. "Fortunately, we've never been really hurt by frost. There's always one part of the vineyard that gets a little bit burned, but it seems to be a different part each year. The crop may be reduced somewhat in those sections that are 'burned,' but not seriously. Of course one of these years we'll have a great big one, that's inevitable. I always figured that once we got into it we'd maybe have one killer frost every ten years or so, but so far we've had no major losses."

Vinifera vines are not vulnerable to dormant-season frosts, or at least the kind that California produces. The only potential problem would be with the freezing of water lines, but by the end of December all the irrigation lines have been drained and the main and sub-main branches are all buried.

In the drought years, Ryan's crew had to contemplate cranking up the irrigation system even before the frost danger had completely receded. With adequate rainfall, as there had been in the early '80s, the creeks would be flowing and the ponds full, and irrigation wouldn't start until late May or early June. In the drought years, it would start in March or even in the winter.

In 1990, after the dreadful year of 1989, irrigation with what water there was began in late March.

Even when there is rain, they still irrigate. The basic rule of California precipitation is that it doesn't rain from May 1 to November 1. "When people who aren't used to California come here in the summer they'll say, 'Boy, it looks so brown, you must be having a really rough summer.' Well, there is never a summer when the hills aren't brown. In Burgundy, they get two inches of rain a month, winter or summer, and mother nature does the irrigation. We can't rely on that. We'd only get half a ton per acre without any irrigation whatever, with total dry farming, compared to the yields that are routinely gotten in Burgundy of three or four tons or more per acre. Even with our supplemental irrigation in the summertime we still get yields below that."

When Calera does irrigate, they irrigate very efficiently and the actual amount of water delivered is small. Their drip system is calibrated to deliver precise amounts per emitter, one gallon per hour to each vine. From May to December they might deliver fifty, sixty or eighty gallons per vine; the maximum they've ever applied, even in the most desperate straits, is a hundred gallons per vine per season, and that was in the 1987 season.

What Jensen hopes 1992's three-hundred-thousand-dollar investment in water will deliver is the ability to give the vines whatever they need, even in the dry years. It's why he plans yet more expenditures—a generator and a large storage tank. "Once we get this dam re-built and see what sort of rainfall we get in the winter, that will give us a handle as to what we might want to buy next year. My hunch is that we'd want a very, very large steel water tank for storing water from our deep wells. I mean two hundred or three hundred thousand gallons, almost one acre foot."

In May, Ryan's crews were in the vineyards spraying for mildew and leaf hoppers, and did one more spraying of herbicides around the base of each vine. In the early years they did all their hoeing by hand, but it was labor-intensive and expensive. By 1990 they were doing a combination of hand-hoeing and spraying.

Through June and July the crews were training the vines, tying up the shoots to the second and third wires. They were shooting rabbits, trapping gophers and ground squirrels, hoeing around the vines and "suckering" the vines, removing the spontaneous growths coming up from ground level or below ground level. If these suckers were allowed to grow unchecked, the vine would be wasting much of its productive energy on growth that served no purpose. The pruners rub off suckers or sprouts on the trunk itself. Those from below ground are followed down to the underground wood system, where they're cut off flush with the trunk. Suckers will come out again in June, when the vine is bursting with new life, and the crews go back and sucker again. The intention is to make sure the vine concentrates on the right kind of foliage and on its fruit.

Once more in late June they went back to repair the deer fence, which had broken in several places.

Several times during the month they disked for weeds. After that, they went at it manually, with a hoe. There was, as there usually is, a "summer" crop of weeds in July.

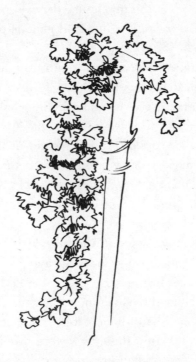

In August, the red grapes "color up." Most wineries take careful note of when this occurs; the process, called *véraison* by the French, is an important part of the season and the French have developed rules of thumb for how many days it is from *véraison* to *vendange*, from coloring-up to picking. Calera takes notes too, but maybe not so carefully. Or in any case, their notes are not always followed very meticulously; nor do they pay much attention to the other Burgundy rule, that there'll be a hundred days from bud break, or flowering, to harvest. At Mount Harlan, *véraison* needs to be tracked mostly because it's a sign that the percentage of sugar in the grapes is increasing, and when the sugar gets up to about eighteen percent of the weight of the grapes, or what the winemakers call eighteen degrees Brix, another of the Gavilan pests, an insatiable bird called the linnet, begins to take an interest.

Ryan's crew breaks out the shotguns again and goes back into the field, trying to scare off the linnets and, where that fails, shooting them. This hardly ever works, because the vineyards are so spread out and inaccessible. Still, they like to try to scare them off before the season starts, to get the population under control before they can do any real damage. Linnets are robin-sized songbirds and the summer cock can be a wonderful wild crimson, but they can eat truly stupendous amounts of fruit, up to half a ton an acre. When yields are four or five tons, this might be acceptable, but in Calera's conditions of unintentional stress management, half a ton can be half the crop and the difference between a profitable year and one the bankers will inherit.

From July to September, therefore, the Calera crews are fighting off pests and watching the grapes ripen.

The picking starts, usually, in mid- to late September.

In 1990, for our bottle of wine in the Jensen vineyard, it started September 17 and lasted until October.

X

*In which when to pick the grapes
is seen to be the most crucial,
and anxiety-inducing
decision a winemaker must make*

From the first of September, Jensen and Ryan were in the vineyards every day, keeping a close watch on the grapes in all the vineyards and their sub-blocks, warily watching the weather and the toll the birds were taking.

When to pick is one of the critical decisions in the life of a wine, and Calera's four vineyards, because of their different grape varieties, slopes and orientations, all mature at slightly different times. The vineyards face all four points of the compass; the western exposure is usually the first to ripen and the north-facing hillsides the last. This makes harvest management easier—crews don't have to get all forty-seven acres in at once. Another advantage: smaller, more flexible crews are needed. The number of pickers can vary from five to ten, depending on the timing and the size of the crop.

Picking can stretch over a full month, usually from September 15 to October 25, though it can vary on either side by several weeks. Calera always picks later than even the coolest portions of Napa or Carneros.

The determining factor in the quality of the vintage is the grape's ripeness.

But when is the grape ripe? When the sugar levels happen to be high? Or is it more complicated than that?

Many winemakers believe that the timing must be very precise and that, particularly in warm climates, the peak period for a crop may last only a few days. That happens only when the raw green tannins have matured and softened but before the acidity goes too low or the sugar too high.

For millennia the traditional way to judge ripeness was to crush a grape in your hand; if the hand remained sticky afterwards, it was time to pick. There are wineries in Burgundy and even in California that pick as much on flavor as sugar, on the taste of the grapes. Taste, however, is a treacherous measuring device and takes great experience to bring off correctly. Grapes in perfect balance are difficult to judge—the acid will hide the sugar and the sugar will mask the acid—and it takes fine judgment to be able to gauge sugar content properly. Josh Jensen doesn't even try. He uses sugar as his main compass, but makes an analytic judgment rather than an aesthetic one. "And then you have to weigh other factors as well. For instance, are the birds starting to get at the vines, is the fruit starting to break down? Pinot noir especially breaks down very quickly."

The pinot noir always ripens before the chardonnay, and the chardonnay before the viognier. Except in 1992, when there was such a heavy crop of the chardonnay that the viognier came in before it.

On September 3, they took a sampling from a part of the Jensen vineyard, Block A, and then samplings from the other blocks of Jensen and the other three pinot noir vineyards. The sample showed low sugar, but it gave them a reading on which vineyard was ripening first. In most years it's the south-facing slope of the Jensen, and indeed, that was the case. Two years later, in the 1992 harvest, the Reed vineyard, for some reason, ripened earliest. "It's usually the latest. I still don't know why this happened. I couldn't believe it. That's why we have only one picking of the Reed '92, not an early and late as we usually do. I kept saying, 'Well, it can't be ripe. It's never been the first to ripen before,' so I sort of held off the picking because I disbelieved the samplings from the vineyard. This year, with the

Jensen, we have four or five batches and with the Mills, we have four or five as well."

As the days went on and the grapes got above twenty percent sugar, these samplings got more and more frequent. Josh and his winemaker, Steve Doerner, worked systematically, going through the vineyard diagonally, taking a representative sample—a big cluster from a vigorous vine, a small cluster from a non-vigorous vine, clusters from different parts of the shoots, from different places on the hillside, some from the top of the hill, some from the thicker soils at the bottom. They also knew that afternoon readings are higher in sugar than morning readings, because during the day the vine is sweating water, whereas at night it soaks it up from the ground. They were also careful to pick whole clusters rather than individual berries. Testing the juice of a single berry is possible, but unrepresentative. The berry's ripeness will depend partly on where it's located on the bunch: riper on the shoulder of the cluster, less ripe at the furthest end from the stem.

They dropped the clusters into a five-gallon plastic bucket, loaded it into Jensen's van and drove down to the winery. There they mashed the grapes and tasted the juice. It looked dreadful, like a purple soup, but it tasted sweet. Then they tested it for sugar content.

There are several sophisticated ways of doing this and two very simple ones. Many winemakers use a refractometer, a device small enough to take into the vineyards. The refractometer is a metal tube rather like a small telescope, with a hinged window at one end. It needs experience to use one properly, because it measures only minute amounts of juice and it's essential to make sure the sample you're measuring really represents the acreage being tested. In the field, you can even squeeze the juice of a single grape onto the window, hold it up to the sun and look into the eyepiece. Light refracts through the film of juice, the sugar content bending the rays, and casts a shadow across a simple-to-read scale.

Jensen, never the chemist, uses the simplest method of all, the hydrometer. This is the most basic measuring instrument in chemistry. You simply pour the grape-juice sample into a little jar and float the hydrometer in it—the higher it floats the more sugar there is. The scale will tell you how much.

The first samples Jensen took read 20.4, meaning 20.4 degrees Brix, or 20.4 percent soluble sugar—not yet ripe enough, although the grapes tasted sweet and showed good color.

They continued taking random samples for several more days.

On September 17, 1990, the Jensen Block A tested at 22.5 Brix.

Jensen radioed up to the vineyard: Okay, let's start picking.

The sampling continued and tests were made on all four vineyards. After two days, when they had picked eight bins of Jensen Block A, the winemakers radioed up to stop picking. "We want to wait a few more days for the middle picking," Jensen told Ryan. "Let's start on the Mills tomorrow."

At Brix 24, picking on the Jensen resumed. Then it stopped again. At 26, Zendejas's crew picked the last batch. It was October 5.

The finished Jensen picking was in four blocks and three pickings. Blocks A and B were combined, Blocks C and D, and Early, Middle and Late pickings of A and B.

This is the way the data were later recorded on winery manager Diana Vita's computer:

A&B Early 420 gallons 13.1 alc 3.66 pH
A&B Mid 720 gallons 13.4 alc 3.71 pH
A&B Late 240 gallons 13.6 alc
Blk C 900 gallons 11.8 alc 3.60 pH
Blk D 240 gallons 12.8 alc

The fourteen-acre vineyard yielded 15.63 tons of grapes. Each ton of grapes gave from one hundred and sixty-five to one hundred and seventy-five gallons of raw new wine.

Jensen doesn't always do early, middle and late pickings. Sometimes he picks only twice, as happened in 1992 with the Selleck vineyard, and, on rare occasions, only once.

Batch picking was an accidental discovery. "We got into multiple picking sort of organically. We evolved into it. Sometimes we'd get sample readings from a particular block that seemed to indicate the grapes were ripe, that they were at twenty-four Brix, so we'd pick a morning or a full day, and find out later it was only twenty-two. So we stopped picking. That would become our early batch. We'd counteract that with higher-ripeness grapes, at maybe twenty-five or twenty-six, and we found that the sum, the combined wine, was in the end greater than its parts. There was vigorous green character from the early picking in the finished bottling and some decadent, rich, almost overdone flavors from the late picking. Put all that together and we found it added diversity and complexity to the wine."

The picking is done by Mexican transient labor, as it is everywhere else in California. Jesus Zendejas is the foreman. "I've been through all kinds of different ways of hiring pickers," Jim Ryan says. "This is the best. Jesus is the foreman of all the laborers, the pruning crew, the other crews. He's full time, works all year, and he brings in all the workers. I tell him I want five guys, he brings me five. I handle the paperwork, but he takes care of the labor."

Jensen says Zendejas "has guys knocking on his door at his house all summer long, reminding him not to forget them when he's putting his picking crew together. People like working for Jesus. He's fair. He expects them to work. If they don't show up one day he doesn't hire them the next. Some years, such as 1992, the pickers were given daily employment for a month, but this was unusual. In 1990 they more typically picked for three days and then stopped for three." (The difference was fifty tons of grapes in 1990 compared to a hundred and seven in 1992.)

The Mexicans pick by hand. The preferred tool is a curved knife, a specialized tool rather like a serrated carpet knife. They're razor sharp. The workers are always sharpening them on their stones.

They work fast, almost at a run. And quietly—except for the occasional shout, curse or laugh. Five-gallon plastic buckets in hand, they tear into the vines and the grapes mound up with amazing speed. The full buckets are dumped into bins carried along on a low flatbed trailer dragged through the vineyards by a tractor. There are two half-ton bins on the trailer; when they're full, they're lifted with a forklift onto the truck that will take them down to the winery. The winery workers will store the whites, the chardonnay and viognier, until the end of the day and then press all the loads in one batch. The single-vineyard pinot noirs, our Jensen among them, are dumped from the trucks straight into the fermentation tanks, each batch kept separate from the others.

In the large valley-floor vineyards, grapes are now often mechanically harvested. Many growers rely on machines to get the crop in quickly, particularly in flat, heavily cropped vineyards of extensive acreage. These machines operate by slapping or shaking the grapes off the vine with plastic beaters. They knock the grapes off the shoots, doing a good deal of damage to the vines in the process. The grapes drop down into conveyor trays and thence to a truck in the next row.

Jensen will have none of this. There are no mechanical pickers in Burgundy although, alas, "progressive" growers are now buying them in some of the lesser appellations of France.

Kermit Lynch, who of all the wine importers and merchants (he's a sometime writer) is most resolutely against new-fangled methods (he once said of himself that he sometimes felt more like a preservation society than a person in the wine business), wrote in *Adventures on the Wine Route* how disappointed he had been one year with the product of one of his once-consistent suppliers. Then he discovered why: the fellow had bought himself a mechanical harvester! "He was tired of dealing with pickers. You must feed them lunch every day, and then there's all the paperwork, because you must treat each harvester as an honest-to-god employee, paying social security to the government, taking out insurance on every one though they only work for a week. And, he believed, no one could tell the difference in the wine. But the wines were thin, without color or aroma."

When Jensen buys grapes for his "workhorse" or mainstay wines, the Central Coast pinot noirs and chardonnays, he specifies to the growers that he'll not accept machine-picked grapes. "A couple of years ago we got a couple of trucks of machine-picked stuff. It was pretty disgusting-looking. We poured it into the tank and it looked like soup, like mush. It didn't smell right. I'm simply prejudiced against it. Of course, if you have a two- or three-hundred-acre vineyard, you can't pick by hand. So we pay a premium for our grapes." In addition, Calera's vinification method calls for fermenting bunches whole, an impossibility with machine-picked grapes. Also, because the grapes are so damaged, they have to be picked at night to avoid too-rapid oxidation and the necessity of over-sulfuring to sterilize the juice.

The truck from the vineyard stops at the barn level, the highest level of the winery. There it's unloaded by a forklift, which takes the bins down one and sometimes two at a time to the crusher level. The bins are dumped into the hoppers, the grapes sliding down a chute into the tanks, a level below.

The last of the 1990 Jensen pinot noir was in its fermentation tanks by October 5.

From this point, the job of the grower was done. Now it was up to the winemakers.

XI

*In which our winemaker reflects
on the risky business of making
wine, and on how dollars can be
even more elusive than quality*

One day in the middle of October, Jensen and I drove to the Iron
Horse winery in Sonoma to take part in an unusual tasting organized
by Riedel, the Viennese glassmakers.

The night before, we'd talked about the wine business and other matters. We started the evening at Toraya, a sushi place in San Francisco's
Japantown. Jensen has catholic, if slightly conventional, tastes in sushi,
favoring concoctions with crab and avocado. We finished a bottle of his
Mount Harlan chardonnay, which he'd brought with him, and then we
repaired for dessert to another of his favorite restaurants, Café Kati. I
remember a marvelous warm pear tart on puff pastry and Jensen's
extravagant raspberry crème brûlée. He drank two glasses of port while
he talked. I finished with a glass of Bonny Doon gewürztraminer ice
wine. We talked for a while about his view of San Francisco as a smug,
small, provincial town. Then, he talked about how he'd undertaken to
get viognier rootstock imported from France, a process that took fifteen
years and rekindled his passionate dislike of bureaucrats of all kinds.

"When I first went to Romanée-Conti, they told me I should come
back a week later when the harvest would begin, so I went down to

Château Grillet, in the Rhône, to help pick there. I took my pay in wine, in three bottles of Château Grillet, the most famous viognier estate. I had gotten to know viognier quite well. The great restaurant La Pyramide, run for decades by the legendary Fernand Point, now deceased, was in Vienne, more or less across the river from Condrieu, and he served Condrieus and Château Grillet, and I tasted viognier there. At that time there were fewer than a hundred acres of viognier in the entire world. Even in France it was rare.

"So in 1971, when I got back to California, I looked around to see if there was any viognier being grown. There wasn't. This was before I owned any land. So in 1973 I paid seventy-five dollars to Davis and their grapevine and plant bureaucracy, the FPMS, the Foundation Plant Materials Service, which is a joint venture between Davis and the U.S. Department of Agriculture, to petition them to start importing viognier vines. There apparently had been some viognier in California in the '30s, but Davis had said about viognier exactly what they'd said about chardonnay—'not recommended for growing in California because its yields are too low.' They were then pushing very high-yielding grapes, like Thompson Seedless, which yielded ten tons an acre but made garbage wine. My seventy-five dollars started the bureaucrat-to-bureaucrat daisy chain. The California bureaucrats contacted the Washington D.C. bureaucrats. Those bureaucrats contacted the French bureaucrats in Paris. The Paris bureaucrats contacted the bureaucrats on the Rhône Growers Council, asking them if they'd let this happen, would they let viognier go to America? So the legal official plants went from the Rhône valley to Paris, from Paris to Baltimore, Maryland, where they were propagated in a USDA quarantine plot to make sure there was no horrible fungus or virus or bug. Maryland finally sent it to Davis and they re-quarantined it there! If you can believe it, it took fifteen years, from 1973 to 1988, before the first bud came out of this bureaucrat-infested pipeline. In the meantime, a couple of people had come and gone who were the heads of the FPMS, and they had no record that I was the guy who started this thing in the first place. Every January I'd call up and say, 'Do you have any viognier budwood this spring?' And they'd say, 'Yeah we do, who are you?' And I'd say, 'I'm Josh Jensen and I started all this,' and they'd say, 'I'm sorry, there's no record of you ... you're not on the list.' I said, 'I started all this! I paid seventy-five dollars!' 'No, sorry, you're not on our list.' Finally they said, 'Okay, we'll let you have some then.' Two or three weeks later they'd call up and say, 'We found a little bit of virus on one leaf so we destroyed it all.' They burned it back to the ground and let it grow back up again. They did this year after year. So in '83, ten years after I started the ball rolling, I heard there was a source in Geneva, New York, so I and La Jota and Ritchie Creek all got our original budwood from Geneva. There was no trouble getting the stuff in from New York. It wasn't strictly kosher, I guess—there is a California quarantine. But the people at Geneva just UPS'd the cuttings to us and we sent them to a nursery. The nursery manager told me later their workers called the vines 'voyager.'"

He started to laugh at the folly of it. Bureaucrats!

Ironically, the viognier plantings were not, initially, a success. The original set of grafts didn't take. "We had some vines that we'd graft and regraft and regraft and they'd grow for a while and die, or never take. We planted two acres in '83, grafted over in '84, regrafted in '85, '86 and '87. We thought we'd get a commercial crop in '87, but we only got a few buckets of grapes from which we made fifty-four bottles. In '88 we made a little over one hundred bottles. But in '89 we had three hundred and four cases, which was two and a half tons per acre. Once we did start getting a crop it's been our Mr. Regular, our biggest yielder, two and a half tons in the first year, then two tons, then two and a half, and this year, 1992, it looks like four tons.

"When we finally got it to market seventeen years after my first petitions, viognier was suddenly fashionable! We found ourselves on the cutting edge! But there was absolutely no forecasting involved, no market research; I just really happened to like this variety and the FPMS farted me around until it became fashionable. "

Bureaucrats indeed. He pushed a little dam of syrup around on his plate for a while, then offered up another example.

"You know that we now have the Mount Harlan viticultural area designation?"

I said I'd noticed it on the label.

"Well, we put a lot of effort into getting that. Actually, we're the only producer in Mount Harlan right now. Know how long it took?"

I said I didn't. But I guessed a year or more.

"Ha! We submitted our application way back in February 1989. It took them a year to get around just to reading our application and then almost another year for reviews and hearings, with final approval being granted December 17, 1990. We've been told we were lucky that the government moved so 'fast' on our application. Seriously!"

"How do these AVAs work?" I asked. "I can see why you want a specific designation. Any Burgundian who believes in soil and the primacy of *terroir* would want it. I know it's the Bureau of Alcohol, Tobacco and Firearms that governs all this, but ..."

"Isn't America wonderful?"

"But, what do you have to demonstrate to them? I've seen BATF described elsewhere as 'omnipotent and sometimes capricious.' How does it work?"

"You must be able to demonstrate to them that the region you want is coherent, makes some distinct sense climatologically, topographically and from a winemaking point of view.

"There are other rules too. They have more rules than you can imagine. Wines labelled with AVA (American Viticultural Area) must have eighty-five percent of their grapes grown in the delimited area. AVAs can be as small as a hundred thousand acres and as large as a hundred thousand."

Calera uses just two AVA designators, Central Coast and Mount Harlan. Central Coast is an immense appellation, including the counties of San Mateo, Santa Clara, Alameda, Santa Cruz, San Benito, Monterey, San Luis Obispo, Santa Barbara and Ventura—think of it as extending from San Francisco south almost to Los Angeles, close to the Pacific Ocean. Calera uses Central Coast to identify wine they use from grapes purchased from other farmers, primarily in the two neighboring counties of Santa Clara and Monterey.

Calera's vineyards currently produce the only grapes in the Mount Harlan AVA—the rest of the land is used for cattle or hunting.

It's somewhat confusing because Calera's "Mount Harlan" vineyards are in fact within the larger area of the "Central Coast." Calera employs, though, the time-honored winemaking, or rather winemarketing, practice of using on the wine labels the smallest and most exclusive appellation to which the wine is entitled.

To explain this in Burgundian terms, the great wines from the small Chambertin vineyard could be labeled and sold under the village name, Gevrey-Chambertin, or, to move down one more notch, as mere bourgogne. Chambertin has that legal right, but it would be folly for them to do it.

In Calera's case, they further accentuate on the Mount Harlan labels the specific names of the four vineyards—Jensen, Selleck, Reed and Mills. Those names are not AVAs, but Calera has trademarked them. For now, Jensen hasn't assigned names to the viognier and chardonnay parcels, though he may some day.

Jensen reached across the table and pulled out one of his mailers, in which he'd quoted a press release from the *California Visitors Review* on the new designation. He started to read: "'Mt. Harlan is a rugged, remote, high elevation area in San Benito County' ... blah, blah, blah ... 'Presently there are only forty-seven acres of vineyard within this large area' ... blah blah ... 'and those vineyard acres are all owned by the small prestigious Calera Wine Company of Hollister.'

"Ha!" he said, interjecting some of his own commentary at this point. "Prestigious! Tell that to the state Water Board!" He propped the mailer against a vase and read on: "'A little known mountain range, the Gavilans form the watershed, and the dividing line, between San Benito County to the east and Monterey County to the west. The new Mt. Harlan area is entirely in San Benito County. This is a high altitude and very rugged area that is mainly used for cattle ranching and for hunting wild boar and deer. The lowest point in the Mt. Harlan AVA is 1,800 feet above sea level, and the highest, the summit of Mt. Harlan itself, is 3,275 feet. Calera's 47 acres of vineyards are planted around the 2,200 foot level.'"

He tucked the mailer away in a pocket. "The first of our wines carrying the Mount Harlan designator was the '87 Selleck pinot noir.

Since ours are the only vineyards in the AVA, for the next six years or so at the very least, and perhaps forever, the words Mount Harlan on a wine label are a guarantee of the very lowest vineyard yields and, hopefully, the highest quality."

I'd noticed that the labels didn't say "Estate Bottled" as some other producers' did. Jensen looked disgusted. "We can't, because of a government regulation that the winery building must be located within the AVA where the grapes are grown, and ours isn't. It's just outside. But if there are wines around that are more estate bottled than ours I'd like to hear of them."

He laughed. "People often ask us why we didn't build our winery close to the vineyards. I point out that there are no paved roads, telephones or electrical service anywhere in the Mount Harlan area. So ... no fax machines, microwave ovens or refrigerators. How could you possibly make wine without fax machines for communicating with your customers, microwaves to heat up your burritos and refrigerators to keep the beer cold during those long hot summer days?"

"What about winemaking as a business?" I asked him. "I mean, premium winemaking, not mass-market stuff. Can you make a living doing this?"

He thought for a while before answering.

"There are so many wineries now not making any money. This is an extremely capital-intensive business and right now, numerous wineries are falling into bankruptcy. Part of the problem is an overcrowded marketplace. Those wineries may be doing everything right, but just can't get shelf space for their products. They just can't get the restaurants to take in yet one more middle-range chardonnay.

"Some of the problems stem from errors.

"Often, people get into the wine business for the wrong reasons. People buying or starting a winery not because they're passionate about it but to have an elegant lifestyle. It sounds so gracious! They build a beautiful house, a luxurious house. They do beautiful landscaping. They hire a chef, rig out a hospitality suite, hire a PR agent. They build a showcase winery. And to do all this they borrow a lot of money from the bank (in the period when banks were

Calera Wine Company

11300 CIENEGA ROAD, HOLLISTER CALIFORNIA 95023

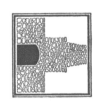

Meg and Les

Thanks

Love

Fran and Peter

Trafton

Return postage guaranteed

looking to lend money—now it's the opposite). So they have high overheads, high costs and a high debt load and can't sell the wine. They then learn a sad truth: premium wineries are capital-intensive businesses that pay back nothing in the short run and sometimes nothing forever.

"It works like this. A doctor, a gynecologist from San Francisco, wants a place in the country, so he buys a few acres up in the hills in Sonoma. Of course, he meets his new neighbors and after a while they say, 'You should put in some vineyards, this is really good land for vineyards here.' And so he does, he plants forty acres of grapes. He sells them to, say, Robert Mondavi or the folks at Sonoma-Cutrer. But his neighbors aren't satisfied. They tell him, 'You're being ripped off by Mondavi (or Sonoma-Cutrer, or whoever), why, they're only paying you fifteen hundred dollars a ton, that comes out to three bucks a bottle and they're selling that wine for eighteen dollars a bottle and you should be getting that eighteen bucks a bottle, instead of the three, they're ripping you off, Joe. You should start a winery like the other people around here and then you could be a winery owner and you could talk about your own wines.'

"And so the poor doctor—or soon-to-be-poor doctor—does that, and suddenly finds himself having to figure out all kinds of new things, all of them with large dollar numbers attached. He has to find distributors. He's got to get himself a winemaker. His winemaker tells him he's got to buy two hundred new barrels each year, at six hundred and sixty dollars a barrel, and that's a hundred and thirty thousand dollars. And suddenly he finds himself in a position where he's losing money every year, year in and year out, a hundred thousand in a good year, two hundred thousand in a bad year. And his problems are structural and unfixable. It's a crowded marketplace and Joe can't just raise his prices. He's got boxes stacking up in the goddamn warehouse, so he's got to cut and discount and deal. Soon he tries to sell the winery, but who wants a losing winery making mediocre chardonnay? So his arcadian dream has led to bankruptcy. And Ernest and Julio buy the winery. They only want it for its vineyards and they get it practically for nothing.

"There's so much discounting going on right now! We recently turned down a two-hundred-case order from a big-shot retailer in Sacramento. We got a phone call from our Northern California distributor's sales manager, and she said this retailer wanted to feature our wines through the Christmas season. Now, for a two-hundred-case piece of business you could take a little something off, but he started trying to nickel and dime us down. It's the nature of today's marketplace. Joe and wineries like his have no choice but to go along, because they have bank payments, property taxes, they must meet their payroll and poor Dr. Joe just doesn't have enough sales revenue coming in.

"We were able to say, 'No thanks, sorry, we thought you wanted the wine, but ...' and we rejected the order."

How did Jensen avoid all those traps? His mournful face dissolved into a grin. He demolished a scaffolding of spun sugar before he replied.

"How did we avoid all that?

"First of all, I managed to keep control of the winery. That's one of the many hazards in a precarious business, that you need money so badly that someone else ends up with control of your operation. Well, I've got news for you, this wasn't a hazard for us. Because no one wanted any part of Calera. It was considered a mongrel operation in a no-name county and no one would invest in it. Even in the San Francisco Bay area people didn't know anything about this part of California. Mention San Benito County in San Francisco and they'll barely know where it is. Mention Hollister and they'll say, 'Oh yeah, Hollister, that's in earthquake country isn't it?' Or they'll say, 'Hollister, isn't that by Eureka?' They've heard of it but don't really know where it is. What we have had for most of our history were vineyards producing uneconomically low yields, we were making a variety that was considered a loser in California, we had people, even family and friends, saying I'd lose my shirt and make a fool of myself over this.

"The standard rule of thumb in the California winemaking business is that you lose money for ten years. And that after huge capital expenditures—vineyards, a large building, tanks, barrels, bottles, everything you need including years and years of expensive labor. The accountants will put those in the capital column and you can get depreciation from them, but the rule is that you lose money for ten years. I was getting money from anywhere I could beg, borrow or steal it. For ten years a little loan here, a little loan there, pledging whatever I could in collateral.

"That standard ten years of losing money was about twelve for us—we bettered it, if that's the appropriate term, by two years.

"There were many, many, many times when it was just so discouraging. It would have been easy just to toss in the towel. But, during those dark and discouraging years, through the middle '80s, our assets if sold wouldn't have begun to cover our debt. I'd have ended up wiped out, unemployed, discredited and branded a failure. So I never did come really close to throwing it in.

"The worst times were at tax time. Now, I never really pay much attention to profitability—I'm not a businessman, an MBA business hotshot type. I operate my business on the basis of personal relationships and a lot of intuition. And so what I've always looked at is our cash flow. In other words, do we have any money in the bank? Can we pay these bills which were due a month ago this week or do we have to wait until next? There've been long periods in our history when we were just not at all prompt at paying our bills. We'd rob Peter to pay Paul. We were really struggling. Every April the accountant would mail me the tax returns and I'd ask him, 'Did we make money last year?' And he'd say, 'No, no, we lost eighty thousand, a hundred thousand, sixty thousand. We got into '84, '85 and '86 and I'd say, 'God, when is it ever going to happen?' And he'd say, 'Well, just keep going, you'll get there in the end.' But it was in that tone of voice, you know, it sounded like he didn't really believe it.

"I remember at one point going over the numbers with my mother, who was then one of my partners, and her accountant, an absolute numbers guy, the kind of guy who didn't very often venture outside his office building in Oakland.

"He mumbled and aahed, and he said, 'Well, let me see if I've got this right, your sales are so and so, and your interest payments are so and so, and your net loss for the year was so and so, sixty thousand dollars?'

"I said, 'Yes, that sounds right.'

"And he said, 'Well, pardon me if this sounds blunt but this doesn't look like a very good business to me. '

"And I said, 'Well, you've said it in a nutshell.'

"And he said, 'So why are you doing this? Why don't you just sell it?'

"And I said, 'Well, um, this is a thing I just gotta do. It'll get there at some point.'"

I was reminded of something George Bain, the Canadian political commentator and wine writer, had once said in *Toronto Life*: "Running a boutique winery," he wrote, "is like joining some religious order fanatically attached to the idea that expiation is achieved only through unremitting toil."

"Yeah," Jensen said, "I can't say it wasn't discouraging, too. I mean, it would be discouraging even if, say, you were a billionaire, a Ross Perot. Ross Perot doesn't want to lose a hundred thousand, year in and year out. It just feels bad. If you're not Ross Perot it feels worse. When you're broke, and you're still borrowing more and getting in deeper and deeper and having to eat crow.

"I guess that's the compulsion that entrepreneurs feel. It can unhinge a person. I've seen it in some people I know. Personal friends as well as some of my distributors. They get to where they get delusional, separated from reality, and persistence becomes obsession.

"In my case, it was a gamble. Pinot noir was immensely unfashionable when I started. Everyone was saying not only was California pinot noir terrible but it always would be terrible. That was the perceived wisdom. So of course when I planted the original twenty-four acres I planted all—only—pinot noir. The gamble was this: I was tasting some pretty good California chardonnays at the time, but almost no pinot noirs that were even interesting, so a successful pinot noir would be great news and a great pinot noir a bombshell. So I put all my chips on pinot noir. I was young enough and dumb enough that I didn't realize I couldn't do it, so I just did it. I just went ahead. I was too dumb to realize I couldn't.

"Now of course they want to know how I knew that pinot noir was going to become fashionable in the '90s, and of course I didn't. I was just nuts about pinot noir. I was just nuts. I still am.

"At some point, though, you must return to reality. If the business really isn't going to make any money, persistence is just delusion. Every year we'd lose money: in '84 eighty thousand, in '85 fifty thousand, in '86 twenty thousand. The losses were getting smaller, the trend was right, but still we'd find ourselves saying, 'Well, we sold a lot more wine this year, why didn't we make money?' Then, in '87, we made a hundred and twenty-five thousand profit. I didn't find this out until '88 and I was dumbfounded when the accountant told me. We've been strongly profitable every year since. And that's with the infernal six-year drought that has taken away half of the highest, profit part of our business.

"Why are we profitable now, when so many others are hurting? I think partly because we acquired and developed the loyalty and respect of our distributors. I had gotten to know and win the respect of and make friends with retailers and restaurateurs all over the country, and our wines got better known. And suddenly, lo and behold, pinot noir started to become at least slightly fashionable and we had finally emerged in many people's opinion as the best, or among the best, in the country, and those who didn't think that we were the best would at least put us in their top five. So our pricing finally got to the thirty-dollar area and our Central Coast wines sold for around fourteen dollars."

Not that all this didn't test his nerves. Pinot noir is a notoriously fickle grape and it certainly teased Jensen. His first crop in 1978 was only seventy-five cases. The Jensen vineyard gave him twenty-two hundred cases in 1987 from a crop of just over two tons an acre. The following year he got a mere four hundred and thirty-seven cases from a crop of less than half a ton per acre. How do you run a business with that kind of unpredictability?

"There are wineries, miracle workers, who can show a profit in their second year by becoming *negotiants*. They don't own vineyards.

They buy batches of wine on the bulk market, they put them out under a *negociant* label or brand, and immediately have sales revenue coming in. And if they buy smart, have a good product and get a good launching into the marketplace, get lucky, they can actually show a profit in their second year. There are guys who bootstrapped operations like that on a hope and a prayer, who have done an enviable job. One brand that comes to mind is called Stratford, which is up in the Napa Valley.

"But they are very much at the mercy of vagaries of the market. If suddenly there's a shortage of chardonnay and they're known for five-dollar chardonnay, and suddenly the cost of chardonnay on the bulk market doubles, they don't even have a business any more. Sales don't just go down, they stop. Because they can't convert those five-dollar-a-bottle customers over to ten-dollar-a-bottle customers."

I asked him to tell me more about the early years of Calera, before his own vines were mature. He sighed, toying with his spoon. Then he used the last of the spun-sugar creation to ladle a small reservoir of syrup into his mouth and pushed back his chair.

He'd finished planting his first three vineyards by the summer of 1975, but it would be a while before he could make wine from his own grapes. It wouldn't be until 1978 at the earliest, and then it would take another year or two before his first Young Vines wines could be released onto the market. His own winery building, the rock-crushing plant, wasn't finished until 1977.

Meanwhile, he wanted to meet other Californians who were producing pinot noir. He also wanted to get started making wine and bring some cash into his business.

By an odd coincidence he found both fine pinot noir and space for rent just on the other side of the Gavilan range, where a winemaker named Dick Graff had set up his business and called it Chalone.

By another odd coincidence, Graff had spent some time in Burgundy and had met and been influenced by the great André Noblet.

Jensen sought him out. "Dick was one of the first people in the industry I met when I came back to California. He was then making *the* great California pinot noir and when I tasted it, out of one of the barrels — and I mean, three or four barrels was all the pinot noir they were making — I said, 'Well, so it *can* be done here.' They were great wines, those late '60s-early '70s pinot noirs from Chalone. It was a small-scale operation, they were strapped for dough, living hand to mouth at that time, but they were doing it right. No redwood tanks for them. I learned a lot from Dick, who has, I think, also learned things from me because I had spent more time in Burgundy than he had been able to."

The Chalone vineyards were only eighteen miles away, on the Pacific slopes of the Gavilan Mountains, and they were just as bleak, just as isolated, just as prone to wild temperature swings of forty or fifty degrees, from intense afternoon heat to chilly evenings, as Calera was to be. André Noblet's influence showed at Chalone too: the soil might be malnourished, rocky, poor — but it did contain limestone.

Like Calera, Graff had problems with water. Anywhere else, Chalone's vineyards would have been classified as desert, and Graff resorted to drilling a well eight miles away on the valley floor near Soledad and running a pipeline up the mountainside. For the first few years Graff eked out a living in the hills, producing five hundred cases of wine a year, without electricity or even a phone line; when he needed to phone for supplies, he used the pay phone at nearby Pinnacles National Monument. In 1972, he found a partner, businessman Phil Woodward, and twenty years later they had grown the business into Chalone Inc., a publicly traded company that owned, among other operations, Edna Valley winery, Carmenet winery and Acacia winery in California, and that entered into a joint venture with Woodward Canyon in the Columbia River Valley in Washington. In 1989, Chalone struck a deal with the Bordeaux company Domaines Barons de Rothschild — the marketing arm of Château Lafite Rothschild and owners of Château Duhart-Milon, Château La Cardonne, l'Evangile and Rieussec — which gave each company a twenty percent stake in the other.

By 1975, when Jensen was looking for winery space to rent, Chalone had built a modern winery but were only using a small part of it, so he rented space from Graff for his first two vintages. This was pure California; no French proprietor would dream of sharing space or equipment in the way California winemakers routinely did and do. In California, winemakers shared everything from equipment to ideas with a candor that would have (and often did) amazed and appalled French winemakers.

This particular circle was completed eight years later when Jensen, in turn, would rent space in his winery, which had been considerably enlarged and expanded the year before and therefore had plenty of space, to yet another idealistic young winemaker-entrepreneur who was trying to get started before having to build a winery, Randall Grahm. Grahm would go on the following year to locate a building in the little town of Bonny Doon, near Santa Cruz, where he had attended university and to name his fledgling winery after the town. Grahm would also go on to become the vanguard of the move on the part of the California wine industry into French Rhône Valley varieties, and subsequently into Italian grape varieties.

However, it wasn't pinot noir that Jensen made from his purchased grapes in this rented space.

"No," he said, making a face. "We bought zinfandel grapes. For our first three vintages, we made only zinfandel from grapes grown by others. So the first wine the Calera Wine Company made was zinfandel. I'd had this idea from the start—we'd make zinfandel at medium prices to keep the cash flowing. The pinot noirs would be our 'art.' We made zinfandel for eleven vintages, through 1985, before we discontinued it."

He was never tempted to plant zinfandel grapes on his own property. And the first year Calera made a profit, '87, was the last year he released any Calera zinfandel wines. The role that zinfandel had been supposed to play in the operation has since been taken by Central Coast pinot noir and Central Coast chardonnay, which Jensen calls his workhorses, his mainstay wines. "These are not inconsiderable wines—nor was our zinfandel—but our single-vineyard wines are a notch above that.

"In hindsight, the zinfandel experience was a big mistake, a strategic error. Hindsight shows zinfandel was starting an historic decline about then and the white-wine boom was in its infancy. If we'd started out making chardonnay and pinot noir, we'd have had our first profit in '82 or '83 instead of '87. We could have ridden the escalator up to high prices, high margins, with much faster product turnover than we got with zinfandel. Zinfandel then as now had an upper limit, a ceiling, to its pricing. Almost no zinfandel can break through the fourteen-dollar ceiling, whereas with chardonnay that would be a midrange price. And you have to hold zinfandel in the barrel longer than you have to hold pinot noir or chardonnay. Bad for cash flow."

In 1975, he made a thousand cases of zinfandel at Chalone, and in '76 two thousand. By the '77 vintage, he'd bought his abandoned rock-crushing plant, and though it wasn't yet ready to make wine, he did make wine on his own property. "We made it up in a pole barn with open sides, which is now our tool shed and dry storage barn. We surrounded it with a cyclone fence because it was open and the bureaucrats required that a winery be lockable." He laughed. "Who was going to steal our stuff up there in the hills?" That summer they worked on the winery; engineers insisted he strengthen and buttress the original walls against earthquake damage. Then they added a fifth, and eventually a sixth, wall at the bottom and enclosed those to be barrel cellars, a warehouse and a bottling room.

In 1978, he hired his first winemaker, Steve Doerner. Doerner had never made a bottle of wine before Josh found him, but that didn't matter. Josh wanted someone with scientific training to help him while he went out to sell his zinfandel and he wanted someone without any preconceived bias as to how wine should be made. Doerner had by coincidence been a student at Davis, but his degree was in biochemistry, not enology. While they both applied Burgundian traditional methods, the simplest, most natural way of making wine, the lowest possible tech, Doerner quickly learned the chemical analyses necessary to try to tip the balance towards more hits than misses.

"That year, 1978, we made wine in our winery, and the year following that I moved from the trailer over to my newly finished house. We were in business."

In the Café Kati in San Francisco, he stood abruptly. "Gotta go," he announced. On the sidewalk outside the restaurant, he waited with me for a cab, then he loped off into the San Francisco night.

In the morning, after dropping off a few things for his daughters at his ex-wife's house and stopping to get some coffee for our drive, we left in his Mr. Pinot van to go to the Iron Horse winery.

As we tooled over the Golden Gate Bridge, I asked him again about the financial aspects of winemaking. He'd just spent huge sums on securing his water supply and had had to postpone buying a badly needed new bottling line because of it—a line that would have cost him another sixty thousand dollars. I knew also that his 1989 divorce from his wife, Jeanne, had been draining, in both emotional and financial terms. The wine business, with its high risks and small, or non-existent, returns for so many years, is hardly conducive to marriage or to any other extended commitment. The divorce is painful to talk about, even now, though he admits its cost. "I was a mess. I had to spend an enormous amount of time on it. It was horrible, and in the process I pretty much neglected Calera."

In the settlement reached early in 1990, Jeanne received part-ownership of Calera, almost a quarter of the business—Jensen's parents had given her some of their share as a wedding present. "That wasn't an ideal situation, running a small private company with your ex-wife," Jensen says, with some understatement. "And I didn't have the dough to buy her out." Selling Calera remained the worst-case possibility, although it was never actually put on the block. In the end, Jensen found a small, locally owned single-branch bank, the San Benito Bank, to lend him the money to buy out his ex-wife, who is no longer involved. The settlement and the resulting interest payments have helped postpone improvements to the winery such as roofs, permanent offices and labs, as well as the new bottling machinery.

His pleasant experience with the San Benito Bank, and his less-than-pleasant memories of much larger banks, have instilled in Jensen another of his business principles: "We try always to do business with small companies. Almost all our distributors are small companies.

Some are *tiny*. We just will not do business with a giant wholesale company, one that sells vodka and gin and every other kind of beverage. We want to work with small, responsive, lean, human organizations in all our business contacts wherever possible."

Despite the crippling interest payments, the winery is now profitable. Jensen is well positioned, with well-regarded wines, a secure water supply and a terrific 1992 harvest, to do well.

"Particularly if we get good rain this year or next. Rain has a double benefit—it fills our reservoir and gives natural irrigation to the vines.

"Look at it this way—seventy to eighty percent of this year's higher yield drops straight through to the bottom line."

To put the 1992 harvest into perspective, two years earlier, in the 1990 harvest that produced our bottle of wine, Calera produced three thousand cases of single-vineyard wines. In 1992 it was seven thousand. The '92 harvest was so good that for weeks Jensen just wouldn't believe the numbers coming in from the vineyard—they seemed too high. "No, that can't be true! That would be two to two and a half tons an acre! Almost up to half of normal California yields!"

The bigger '92 harvest could bring in about eight hundred thousand in additional sales revenue, on a '91 base of less than two million dollars—a substantial increase by any standards. The only incremental costs are additional labor, many additional barrels to keep the wine in and the extra packaging costs, fairly high at around fifteen dollars a case—additional bottles, corks, capsules, labels, palettes, tissue paper for wrapping. But of the eight hundred thousand dollars in additional revenue, only a hundred thousand or a hundred and fifty thousand or two hundred thousand might be cost; the rest goes directly to the bottom line.

Would one of the options be to use the money to plant more vineyards? "I'd like to, sure. I'd like another hundred acres. If we could get to fifteen thousand cases from our own vineyards, that would be great; that's a good size. Profitable, but not so big as to demand different ways of running the business. This means big bucks, though, probably better than a two-million-dollar investment." And maybe outside investors: mountainside acres cost about twenty-five thousand each to bring to full production exclusive of land costs, and without a long string of exceptional years, the winery couldn't sustain the investment.

An hour or so later we turned into the driveway at the Iron Horse winery, located on three hundred acres of rolling countryside in Sonoma's Green Valley. Iron Horse produces some pinot noir, but specializes in sparkling wines under its own label. The working buildings of the farm are small and functional, but the farmhouse is a gracious, rambling structure more than a hundred years old, surrounded by lovingly tended gardens. The tasting was held on a patio near the winery, a pleasant nook under an arbor overlooking the vineyards. The October sunshine was warm and golden. It seemed an idyllic spot and an idyllic life. It was easy to see why urban refugees could be seduced into trying it.

Iron Horse was founded by Barry and Audrey Sterling. Barry was a Los Angeles lawyer with a practice on both coasts and in Paris and a taste for the good life, almost as if he were the prototype for Josh Jensen's story of how to go broke making wine. Just as in the story, he fell in love with Sonoma's gentle hills and set about restoring a rundown property. However, he avoided the trap Josh had outlined, partly by making excellent wine. He also had the good sense to have a daughter, Joy, who became a winemarketer of superior skill. She had the further sense to marry another winemaker of ability, Forrest Tancer, Barry and Audrey's original partner. Iron Horse produces first-rate sparkling wine, and has recently gone into a joint venture with Laurent Perrier of France. They use the *méthode champenoise*; but while the *méthode* may be *champenoise*, the technique is pure American: the champagne bottles are given the careful and requisite one-eighth turn every few hours not by highly trained cellar workers but by a clanking machine capable of turning four hundred bottles at a time. The bottling operation, on the other hand, is curiously low-tech and depends heavily on the ability of one of the workers to get his thumb over the bottle mouth with sufficient rapidity not to lose any wine as the crown cap is flipped off, the fermenting syrup inserted and the bottle corked.

For this day, Joy had brought together four premium producers of pinot noir—Acacia, Iron Horse, Calera and Saintsbury—at the suggestion of the Riedel glassware company representative, who had a point to make. The wines were Acacia's '86 St. Clair, Iron Horse's '87 pinot noir, Calera's '91 Central Coast and Saintsbury's Reserve '90. The tasting was unusual in that we were not to compare wines but the glasses they were poured into.

The glass, Georg Riedel said in a little introductory lecture, is just another tool in the winemaker's armory. He maintained that the "profile" of the glass, by which he meant its depth-to-circumference ratio, its capacity and whether the wine pours from it in a wide arc or a narrow lip, makes a difference to the way the wine tastes. Different glasses will show, or mask, different characteristics of the wines, he said. Some glasses would bring out the acidity in the wine, some the fruit, depending on where in the palate the effect was felt and on the shape of the "pour." We were to drink the same wine from four different glasses and make notations on a tasting sheet. Afterwards, we would see if he were right.

It's fair to say that his little lecture was received with a good deal of skepticism, though everyone was too polite to say so. They sipped diligently from the four glasses on the table—the Vinum Burgundy White (small and tulip shaped, twelve and three-eighths oz.), the Sommelier's Montrachet (squatter, less tapered, seventeen and five-eighths oz.), the Vinum Burgundy Red (more bulbous tulip, and bigger than the White, twenty-four and three-quarters oz.) and the Sommelier's Burgundy Grand Cru (a thirty-seven-ounce behemoth that to my taste was clumsy and much too large, but which some of the others liked).

Everyone slurped and spat, pouring the surplus wine into the gravel under the bench. From time to time, they'd scribble on their sheets. Afterwards, we compared notes. My own tasting notes were far from precise, but to my surprise even I could tell that some wines did better in some glasses than in others. Most of the winemakers present were astonished, and while there was no real consensus, there was clear agreement that Georg Riedel's notions had been generally right. What did it mean, though? That careful winemakers could move more product by stocking a wider variety of glasses in their tasting cellars? That yet another level of complexity should be added to the experience of consuming fine wines? Or was it just a curiosity, to be noted and forgotten?

Afterwards, we went to lunch at the main house, prepared by the winery's chef, and then set off for San Francisco and south, back to the Calera winery.

XII

*In which the grapes come in
from the vineyard to start their
magical transformation into wine,
and in which techniques are described*

The grapes from the Jensen vineyard, Early Picking, Block A, went roaring past us down a stainless-steel chute and plunged into the open-topped fermentation tank, six feet below. The Block B grapes would follow in a few days. I noticed a few leaves, though not many, and also that the berries were still on their stems.

A week or so earlier, at one of the California wine shows, I'd interrupted Jensen as an earnest young wine-buyer was asking him about this business of stems. Did he destem at all? the young man wanted to know. If he didn't, were the stems woody-brown or green, and would that make a difference? Jensen was replying patiently, but I dragged him away, needing him for some other purpose. The young man glared at me. I ignored him.

Clearly, Calera didn't destem its grapes. There wasn't a destemmer anywhere in sight. I asked Josh what the orthodoxy on the matter was. The theory behind removing the stems was that they contributed too much astringency and bitterness to the finished wine if fermented with the grapes. He'd used a destemmer for a portion of each tank-load until 1984. After that, the percentage of destemmed grapes gradually declined to zero; he put whole bunches into the fermenter, not even crushing them, just punching them down a bit to break some of the skins. "I now think the destemmer bashes up the stems and extracts more astringency than if you leave the bunches alone," he said.

Another bin was tipped and the grapes slid past us into the fermenter. Eight feet or so tall, the tank was already about half full. A few more bins and they'd move to another fermenter.

There's no consensus on this matter of stems. Dick Graff at Chalone does as Jensen does, using whole clusters with the stems on. But Larry Brooks, the winemaker at Chalone's sister winery, Acacia, destems and crushes the bunches gently before fermentation starts, leaving about a quarter of the bunches whole. Tim Mondavi, at Robert Mondavi wineries, used to leave the stems on but has now reverted to destemming; he believes the stems "give some spice to the wine, but dry them out too fast as they age." Kent Rasmussen, a young winemaker with his own eponymous winery, who makes some very fine pinot noirs, destems a little more than half the grapes.

"So it's not just Davis that says take the stems off?" I asked.

Jensen laughed. "No. Now, I don't ..."

"I know," I said. "You don't want to be a Davis-basher, but ..."

"... want to be a Davis-basher at all. I'm not nearly as anti-Davis as I sound."

We wandered across to his house, set like the winery on cascading levels down the steep hillside, and settled around a table on the lowest level, overlooking the rolling hills of the Gavilan range. I asked him to tell me what he really thought of the Davis school and its theories of winemaking. Clearly, they'd done plenty of good for the industry, if only in the vineyards. Many of the techniques they had discovered, such as deep-ripping the land, were now routine practice in vineyard operations, including Calera. Their "foundation plant" sciences section, where they mutated, cloned and tested dozens of different grape varieties in small plots, had been derided by some winemakers as concentrating too much on yield and not enough on quality and flavor, but had nevertheless taught all winemakers much about plant biology and its pathologies. That California vineyards were as healthy as they were had much to do with Davis, the contentious reoccurrence of phylloxera notwithstanding.

The main quarrel with the school, as far as I could see, was the suspicion that since it was funded largely by massive Central Coast bulk wineries, the school's basic assumptions favored high yield and consistency of flavor over character, nuance or "ageability." The emphasis was on mass production, on what the French call *vin technologique*. Everything had to be air-tight, squeaky clean. Kermit Lynch once wrote scornfully of some hapless winery that "the Invasion of the Enologists is [the horror film] now playing at their local cinema ..."

Josh Jensen agrees with this, though he gives it all a more charitable spin. "When Prohibition ended, most of the American industry had been locked up and shut down for twenty years, and to a certain extent they'd forgotten how to make wine. So the University of California at Davis was instrumental in fighting hard and encouraging the industry to make sound, safe wines and not vinegar through the meticulous application of the scientific method—primary chemistry, tightly controlled fermentation, meticulous sanitation and heavy filtration. They were adamant in taking very conservative, cautious approaches. In the large scale this was a good thing, because without it there would have been a lot of unsound, spoiled wines. To their credit, the result was a preponderance of sound wines, cheap, homogeneous jug wines, but still sound.

"On the other hand ... they preached an interventionist, control-everything type of winemaking, consistent with a basic belief that technology can solve all problems, and you just can't make great wines that way. Why? Because no attention is paid to the characteristics of the grape, or the soil, or to excellence or to the very idea of extraordinary quality." High-technology winemaking is salvage winemaking—it's for saving wine that has gone wrong or was never very much right in the first place.

"So," I asked, "they believed if they understood enough of the wine's chemistry, that if they got just the right clone, the right fermentation temperatures, the right yeast strain, the right stainless-steel tank and sterile filters and centrifuge, they could produce great wines?"

"Well, the school's mandate was not great wine. Their graduates, some of whom did want great wines, believed more in microorganisms than in character. You can't make great wines if your focus is on killing microorganisms. You can make interesting wines, but not wines of the very first rank.

"Most of those industrial-style wines lacked color, lacked complexity and lacked character—safe and boring. This conservative approach will do this with whatever grape you're using, but especially with pinot noir."

Pinot noir's most important claim to fame is its silky softness and heady perfume. But while it can have wonderful undertones of plum and damson richness, pepper and honey, it can also be tough, sullen, intense or jammy. Sometimes it seems to veer between all these with unnerving suddenness.

Jensen calls it the "especially" grape. "Because whatever you can say about wine and winemaking, and about any grape, you can always say, 'and especially pinot noir.' Hard to get good color in red wines? Especially pinot noir. Difficult to get a good yield from a vineyard? Especially pinot noir. Too much racking takes color and flavor from the wine? Especially from pinot noir. Clones are important for good grapes? Especially with pinot noir. Same with 'Soil is important' and 'Traditional procedures are important' and 'Racking and filtration take a lot of color out.' "

It was left to the next generation of American winemakers, such as Josh Jensen, to reject this notion of wine as some kind of malleable Pygmalion to be made over by white-coated Henry Higginses, and to rediscover the surprises and pleasures of minimalism, formerly known as nature. And minimalism—when to leave well enough alone—is an acquired skill. Anyone can make pretty good wine; to learn the patience of great wine takes a lifetime.

We wandered back over to the winery; another truckload of grapes was coming in from the vineyards and Jensen wanted to be there. "Here's what I really think about winemaking," he said, ticking off the points on his fingers. "The grape essentially knows what to do. The job at the farm level is to get the grape to the perfect state and capture it at that moment. And then the winemaker's job is to stand in the background, get out of the way and let it get into the bottle as purely, as naturally, as possible, with as little done to it as possible. When in doubt, don't do it. Too much California wine is made from a standard recipe. It's why they had so much trouble with the pinot noir grape before. You can't treat the pinot noir that way."

I thought this doctrine of rigorous non-interventionism somewhat disingenuous and said so. He looked sheepish. "Well," he said, "there are times when you have to intervene. If someone gets a headache you have to give him aspirin. The point is, when in doubt, do as the Burgundians do, that's your starting point. And they do as little as possible."

We went back up to the fermentation tanks and peered in. The tank was three-quarters full of grapes, most of them still whole but a small percentage broken open. It smelled, of course, nothing like wine but of crushed fruit and bruised wood.

"Okay," I said, "here's our single-vineyard pinot noir–to-be, the Jensen Mount Harlan pinot noir. You're going to charge thirty dollars a bottle for this stuff. How do we get from this"—I gestured at the purple stew below—"to that bottle? What do you do? And what would Davis do differently? What were they doing wrong when they called the pinot noir the heartbreak grape?"

Josh stared into the sky for a minute or so, mentally sorting his lists. Then he started checking them off:

"I've already told you quality has first of all to come from the vineyard—where to plant is the first crucial decision.

"First of all ... the disappointing pinot noirs of the bad old days were made from grapes planted in too hot an area—the grapes lacked color, acidity and balance. Probably they were overcropped— the winemaker was taking five tons to the acre instead of two. And then, of course, they were paying no attention to soil. This is the most important. They weren't planting on limestone soil. Even in Burgundy, once you get off the limestone ridge and out on the flats, you don't plant pinot noir, you plant gamay. It's going to make an ordinary wine down there anyway, so you plant gamay to have even more ordinary wine. It's the small differences in the soils between one parcel and another that explain the differences in the characters of the wines. So: plant vines in the right place and keep their yields low. Those are the main things. Do all the others if you must: develop pruning and training techniques, irrigate properly, do canopy management, leaf removal, stress management by 'deficit moisture' and the rest, but those are the important ones.

"And then what we do: keep the vineyard parcels separate, do batch pickings of early, middle and late, and consolidate these later."

"So in fact you intervene all the time?"

"Yes, but not in the sense that Davis means it. We intervene to help the natural process. We're really lucky today. We can still make wine the way they did at the turn of the century, but with our technology we can detect problems early and take care of them when they arise. Look, there are perhaps a thousand decisions that have to be made in a wine's life—up to the time it gets into the bottle. After that, there are really no decisions left, except for labels and capsules and the like—most of these decisions are tiny; maybe ten are of huge importance, crucial.

"So a winemaker can be a hired gun, to help make all those decisions. Or the winemaker can make five hundred of them and the owner make five hundred, or somewhere along that scale. The decisions range from the most minor—when to wash and scrub the floors, what type of bucket to put the wine in, moving the wine from one barrel to another—to, when do you sulfur the wine, how often do you test it for vinegar, what do you do if you get a vinegar bacteria growing in one barrel but not in another? And so on. How much sulfur? For how long? Do you filter? Are you going to bottle when it's twelve months old, fifteen months old, twenty-four months old? Those are some of the decisions.

"Here's a simple example: at first, I intentionally picked our pinot noirs at low sugars to keep the alcohol level of our wines low, around twelve percent, because I didn't want them top-heavy, clumsy—I wanted elegance. But my friend Aubert de Villaine from Romanée-Conti tasted our new '82s from barrel and said they were our best yet. When I told him they were higher in alcohol, around thirteen percent, than we'd previously made them, he replied, "Oh, of course, pinot noir has to have at least thirteen degrees of alcohol to get the right fullness of flavor." So from then on we left the grapes to mature longer on the vine. That led to riper, richer grapes, and to the richness and big structure that our wines have become known for — while still possessing a certain elegance. We try to accomplish that without allowing the grapes to overripen, which would give the wine what Burgundians call *gout de brûlée*, a raisiny burnt flavor. This was a decision I had to make, not the winemaker, to set the style for our wines. Typically, I participate in all the big decisions. Steve, and now Sara, do absolutely all the day-to-day winemaking. I've been more active recently, trying to assist Sara in her transition, to help her understand what we do and what they do in Burgundy, because she's never made pinot noir before. But she's a very sound, talented, very competent person, and a big part of her job is the scheduling of the workmen, at the presses today, fill these barrels tomorrow ... use this barrel for this batch, and so on.

"Of course I have the final say. It's like the famous Abraham Lincoln quote after a cabinet meeting: 'There are eleven nays and one aye; the ayes have it ...'"

I interrupted. "This, of course, means that first of all you have to know where you want to go, what kind of wine you want to make ..."

"Of course, yes. The whole process of winemaking starts with a basic directive — what do you want the wine to taste like? You have a goal and you want to maintain that. Much of our intervening, a lot of the analysis Sara does, is to help protect this vision — to protect the wine from spoilage or to verify a flavor, something as simple as when the grapes come in how sweet are they, are they sweet enough? There's a lot of flavor development you can just taste, but if you can get an actual reading, so much the better."

We wandered down into the barrel-storage area and then into the trailer that serves as an office and lab. Sara Steiner was bent over a Bunsen burner. We left her alone and went out to the driveway, staring across at the Gavilan hills and down into the San Andreas Fault.

"Poor Sara. She arrived here in August ten days before we started our crush, the absolutely busiest time of the year for a winery. Bad timing on our part. She arrived for her first day of work August 10, and we immediately started bottling the '91 Central Coast pinot noirs. We'd very brilliantly, with a lot of thought going into it, planned the Central Coast pinot noir bottling, the biggest batch we'd ever made, about ten thousand cases, so it would all be done before the crush started. Wrong! Last year the crush started on October 7, three weeks later than normal. This year it was three weeks earlier than normal, six weeks earlier than last year. Grapes started arriving August 20, when we had only just gotten started bottling the pinot noirs.

"So we found ourselves in a bind. Everyone else in California was in the same situation. They were all bottling when the crush started. In addition, our glass supplier ran out of glass, our cork supplier couldn't get us the corks we wanted and the label people couldn't get us the labels in time, so we kept running into these delays, which meant we were going to be bottling later and later into the crush. Oh, it was a great time for a winemaker to start at a new place. Sara and the winery guys worked from seven a.m. to at least ten at night for four straight weeks, not even an afternoon off during that time, pressing, putting the wine into storage tanks, into barrels, keeping the counts right, making sure there was the correct number of new barrels and old barrels for each batch of wine, and so on. It was hairy."

"Okay," I said, "but come back to this matter of what you do to the grapes after they're in the winery, until they're in bottle. What are the decisions you must make?"

He resumed his mental list.

"First, what yeast will ferment your grapes? Are you going to speed up the clarification of the new wine afterwards? How long do you ferment and at what temperature? What do you do about the sediment, the lees? What do you do about acid and sugar content? You have to manage the cap that rises to the top of the fermentation. There are decisions about pressing. How long to let the wine settle? How long to keep in barrel? How, and whether, to get a secondary or malolactic fermentation? How long to store and keep, and in what? Whether to remove the sediment. Whether to filter or to fine, or both. When to bottle. How long to keep in bottle. What to drink in the long, long, meantime ..." He grinned.

I leaned over to look into the fermentation vat. The grapes had settled some, but not much. The bunches at the bottom were being broken by the weight of fruit above them. The winery was making no effort to break them up.

"Doesn't look as if anything is going on in there," I said. "What in fact is happening, if anything?"

"At the moment, not very much. First thing in the morning, we'll add acid to the must, the fermenting juice ..."

"I thought you didn't intervene?"

He looked impatient. "In California we virtually always add acid to our pinot noirs. Our climate is warmer than Burgundy's, and we can almost always obtain full ripeness in the grapes every year. We can get our grapes at twenty-four percent sugar, which is going to make a rich, potentially dark, full-bodied, full-flavored strong wine. In Burgundy they can't always do that. There, the great years are the hot, dryer years, when the vines ripen their grapes up to twenty-four percent sugar, but many years it starts to rain September 1 and it rains all month and they have a big mess on their hands. They have to pick at twenty percent sugar, or twenty-one, or nineteen. So they are allowed to add sugar to the juice, a process called chaptalization.

"In California, it's just the opposite. We never have to add sugar — we couldn't anyway because it's illegal — but we don't have to in any case. But we almost always add acid to end up with a balanced wine. The cheap way is to use citric acid, which doesn't cost very much, but you should never do that with good wines. First, because it gives the wine a citric flavor, and then because citric acid is not as stable. We add the acid that's the primary acid of grapes to begin with, tartaric, which is very expensive. About two hundred dollars for a hundred-pound bag of it, and we add bags and bags and bags of it. But, you know, again ... if you want to play with the big boys, don't try to economize on the essentials."

"How do you know how much to add?"

"How much? That's part of what Sara's doing now. We always add the acid within twenty-four hours of the grapes going into the fermentation tanks. We look at total acidity as well as pH, which are two ways of expressing acidity. When we get a low-acid (high pH) reading, we add acid. In the lab, Sara will see how many grams of acid per liter of juice she needs to bring the pH down to 3.4, or something like that. That calculation determines how many bags of tartaric we need to add."

Later, I asked Steiner what the procedure was. "You can take samples as the grapes come in or as we punch it down and mix it. What I do is to try to really accurately gauge the fruit, and then add the acid right away. We want to do this to the grapes and not to the wine. We try not to manipulate the wine's chemistry, so we do it during fermentation. And then, while the wine's fermenting we constantly test the dropping sugar levels.

"We harvest our grapes really ripe, and as pinot noirs ripen they tend to lose acidity. Pinot noir is notorious for the pH readings going very high and the acidity dropping out as the fruit ripens. Or dropping out during fermentation."

So far it didn't seem very non-interventionist to me. In Burgundy they add sugar, in California they add acid. Would Jensen add sugar if he needed to? Assuming it were legal? He said he'd probably do some trials with it if the practice were ever legalized, as it is in Oregon. "My hunch is that it's not the key. Everybody wants to find the key to the Burgundian mystery, but I don't think that's it. I think the real key is limestone soil."

In the morning, we were drawn back to the big tub of grapes on the fermentation level. I peered in again. Still nothing much seemed to be happening. This was slightly misleading. Deep in the must, where the berries had been broken by the weight above them, yeast spores were beginning to feed on that twenty-four percent sugar. They were just beginning the population explosion that in a few days would turn the vat into a seething mass of purple muck and foam. It's at this point that Josh Jensen and the other pinot noir specialists start to really part company with the California norm.

In all vineyards, on every grape and every bunch there are native airborne yeasts. When left entirely to itself, therefore, grape juice will naturally ferment by the action of these yeasts. Alas, other airborne microorganisms are less desirable—for the winemaker, the vinegar bacterium is the most sinister. The normal California practice is not to take chances. They therefore add sulfur dioxide to the must in sufficient amounts to kill the native yeasts as well as all presumed harmful microorganisms, then immediately "inoculate" the must with cultured yeasts. Sulfur dioxide or SO_2, has been the primary weapon of winemakers for centuries: it's an anti-oxidant, a bactericide and, thus, a preservative. Most winemakers, Jensen included, believe they couldn't make wine without it—in the very small doses in which it is normally employed.

Some of these wonder yeasts are proprietary to the wineries that developed them, like the "Woodbridge," developed by the Mondavis, a low-foaming yeast suitable for barrel fermentations. Others were developed in France and in the labs of Germany, and include Montrachet, possibly the most popular, which is used for reds and whites; it tolerates sulfur dioxide better than most, but it doesn't work well with high-sugar grapes and can be slow. Pasteur red, or French red, is a mixed-population strain developed in the Bordeaux region; it tolerates heat and sulfur and rarely 'sticks', or stops fermenting. Assmannshausen from Germany is used mostly for zinfandel and pinot noir, because it intensifies color and imparts a spicy fragrance, but it's not suited for must with high solids, like Calera's.

Jensen is scornful of these products, and of American determination not to let nature takes its course. Other high-end winemakers, like Larry Brooks of Acacia and Jim Clendenen of Au Bon Climat, do use cultured yeasts, and they typically refer to the ones that come with the grapes as "wild yeasts." "Call them native yeasts please," Jensen insists. "Americans are so apprehensive about using native yeasts they even call them wild." He calls the cultured yeasts "washday miracle yeasts."

"You kill everything with big doses of sulfur dioxide and then you put in a super-miracle product you've bought at your super-miracle chemist's supply shop, using vigorous, but highly selected propagated yeasts to do a clean, fast fermentation instead of the slower, sequential native yeasts. You're just not going to get the same quality."

Still, in addition to the acid, Steiner had added a small (sub-critical to yeast) dose of sulfur dioxide to the grapes to try to inhibit "spoilage organisms" (a.k.a. vinegar) that might interfere with a clean fermentation. She explained it this way: "Yeasts are incredibly tough. They can take higher sulfur levels than vinegar. They also metabolize a lot of that sulfur, so by the time fermentation is finished there might not be any sulfur left. So the sulfur inhibits deleterious bacteria initially and allows the yeasts to make a clean fermentation."

For the next while, nothing much seemed to be happening in the fermentation vat. No one seemed troubled by this. This passive phase can sometimes go on for two or three days. If it lasts four days, concerns are raised, but this is very unusual. After all, pinot noir juice is an almost perfect fuel mixture for yeast. Crushed pinot noir grapes have been known to ferment overnight, and to get the most out of the grapes, winemakers must attempt to slow the fermentation down. This is one reason for the whole bunches: the yeast can't get at the sugar inside the berries, so the fermentation takes longer. This is also one of the reasons you want the stems, which are non-fermentable, in the must: they dilute the mix and thereby slow things down.

Sometime in the third day, small foamy bubbles appeared on the surface of the must, a first sign that yeast cells had finished multiplying and were beginning their real job, converting sugar to alcohol and carbon dioxide. The vat began to give off the characteristic fermenting odors, a heady mix of carbon dioxide gases and grape aromatics. This is one of the most reassuring smells in the world to a winemaker; it's a sign that matters are proceeding as they should.

The vat also began giving off considerable heat as a fermentation by-product. Heat is a concern.

The Davis red-wine recipe calls for prolonged, cold fermentation. Cold fermentation is safe fermentation—yeasts begin to die at temperatures of ninety-two degrees Fahrenheit and higher, and since fermentation, being exothermic, can generate considerable heat, musts can easily shoot up to ninety-five or a hundred degrees. Then, as Jensen puts it, "you could have a great big mess on your hands, a stuck fermentation, and you can't just toss in some yeast, because the yeast won't propagate in an environment that has significant alcohol in it, so you have to then 'bleed' the stuck wine slowly into an active fermentation in another tank—if you have one." Cold fermentation brings out the fruit in wines, while hot fermentation gives fullness and gutsiness, what Jensen calls "vinous qualities."

"Cold fermentation will give you fruit-juice flavors—not soda pop, but fruit juice. Warmer fermentation will give you wine characteristics, vinous flavors. So pinot noir should be fermented at a high temperature, as they do at Romanée-Conti. This is high-risk winemaking, but if you're going to attempt to scale the heights, to attain that ultimate last few percentage points of quality, you need to do it that way, take those risks."

It's critical, therefore, to watch the temperature. Calera's stainless-steel fermentation tanks, which range from a thousand to six thousand gallons capacity, are jacketed with a hollow outer casing in which cold water can be circulated to cool the must. As soon as the temperature gets up to hazardous levels, these "chillers" are turned on to knock it down. The danger point is usually thought to be around eighty-nine or ninety.

Jensen likes his fermentations at about eighty-five or eighty-six degrees. "It'll get up to eighty-nine, we'll knock it down to eighty-two, eighty-three, it'll go back up to eighty-six. We like to have it up there near the red line. We're looking at it the whole time and will turn the chillers on for an hour or two at a time. The main problem is the temperature can spike up overnight. The sugar is the fuel in the fire here. By the time it gets down to fifteen, sixteen percent sugar, the fermentation is really flying and that's when there's plenty enough fuel to shoot the temperature up really high, so that's when you have to watch it closely. If on the other hand the tank is eighty-six degrees and there's only four percent sugar left, that's not enough to push it up to the danger point."

One of the hazards of hot fermentation is increased risk of vinegar. "Vinegar bacteria are carried on fruit flies, and they're going to be in every tank of wine, and as careful as you are you're going to see higher levels of acetic acid in warm-fermented wines. If all goes well, though, and you practice good sanitation, it's not that much higher."

I asked Josh why he didn't ferment his pinot noir in oak tanks. Wasn't that the Burgundy tradition? It was, he said, but not any longer. Romanée-Conti uses all stainless steel now, and so do the other Burgundy houses that can afford it. "Stainless is the material of choice. For the two weeks that red wine is fermenting in a tank, you don't extract any flavor from the oak anyway, especially because most of the oak fermentation tanks are so old now that any oak character or flavor would have long disappeared. Basically what you want for a fermenter is a neutral, easy-to-clean, vessel."

Neutrality? I found it hard to say "neutral" and "Jensen" in one breath. "Risk" seemed a better fit. But I guessed there were risks enough in what he was doing.

XIII

*In which grape juice transforms itself
into wine, and the arcane subjects
of oak barrels and secondary
fermentations are discussed*

The red foam that appeared on the surface of the new wine was caused by carbon dioxide gas. After a few days, when the must was fizzing, the gas pushed the suspended skins and stems to the top of the tank. In a while this "cap" became quite thick, solid enough to stand on. Managing the cap is one of the primary tasks of the winemaker. But how—by "punching down" or by "pumping over"?

It may seem like a trivial decision, since either way the purpose is the uncomplicated one of keeping the cap moist. If it dries out, the skins could become infected with vinegar bacteria. And if the skins are piled up on top of the juice, you won't extract as much color, flavor or tannin as you could. "Grape skins are where the coloring matter is," Jensen says. "And much more—the phenolics, the aromatics, the flavoring matter, all reside in the skin, not in the juice. But particularly color. Color is Job One with pinot noir. So doing the right thing with that cap is one way of getting a dark wine when the wine doesn't want to be dark."

So keep it moist. But how? The cap is a sort of giant teabag floating on top of the juice; you can moisten it by using a circulating pump to shift wine from the bottom of the tank to the top of the cap, or you can plunge the cap into the tank. The first, pumping over, is the Bordeaux way. But it won't get as much color from the skins as punching down will. For cabernet and virtually all the other varieties, you have color to spare, so you can risk it. But pinot noir is deficient in color. In Burgundy, therefore, the preferred method is to plunge the cap down into the juice, using a plank on a pole or the human foot, which is perfectly adapted to the task.

Punching this cap down can be hard, even backbreaking work. The thing is *heavy*! But it must be done, at least twice a day as Calera does it, or six or seven times a day as other wineries prefer. Calera has come up with a technological solution and has rigged up a pneumatically powered piston with a stainless steel plate at the bottom that slides along an I-beam just above the fermenters. It runs on air pressure. One man can operate it, sliding it along the beam from one tank to the next to plunge the cap, a small portion at a time, to the bottom of the tank.

The active fermentation takes a few days to start and may continue for a week or longer. Our Jensen 1990 sat in its fermentation tank for fifteen days. For the last three or four of those days, very little was happening, but Jensen likes to leave the skins in contact with the juice for a few extra days—the additional time increases fruit flavors and the perfume. Other high-end producers of pinot noir do the same thing. Tim Mondavi, for example, sometimes leaves the juice in contact with skins as long as twenty-eight days. At Saintsbury, they average sixteen to eighteen days.

It's a question of balance. The main influences on wine's flavor are the skins of the grapes, the yeasts used to ferment, the deposits of dead yeast cells after fermentation, and the container used in making and storing the wine. The fermentation part of the process must get the best out of the tannins, and the coloring and flavor elements in the grape, and achieve a balance between tannin, fruit, alcohol and acid.

Two weeks and a day after the grapes came down from the vineyard, they were fully fermented, no longer grapes but dry, still mucky-looking raw wine, the sugar levels down to vanishing point and the yeasts dead from lack of nourishment after their great binge ("belching carbon dioxide and farting alcohol," as a farm worker once put it when I was a kid). The valve at the base of the tank was opened and the new wine was allowed to drain through a screen and then into a temporary storage tank one level below. This is called the free-run wine. The residue—the muck of grape skins, stalks, wilted leaves and dead yeast cells—was scraped through a hatchway at the base of the fermentation tank directly into the press, which had been wheeled over to receive it.

This press looked to me nothing like the old basket presses I'd been used to as a boy. Those rather more romantic old devices somewhat resembled oak barrels with half the staves missing, with an oaken plate that screwed down on the pomace, as the must residue is now called, squeezing the remaining juice through the slats on the sides and down into a small gutter, whence it was led to barrel.

Calera's presses are probably their highest-tech devices. Gleaming stainless-steel horizontal cylinders, they look rather more like smaller versions of milk-delivery tankers than anything to do with wine (or, it occurred to me later, like massive versions of those devices that keep mediocre food warm in steam trays at serve-yourself restaurants).

The white wines—the chardonnays and the viognier—which don't ferment in contact with their skins go directly from the vineyard into either the larger Willmer Presser or the smaller Europress. The red, both the Central Coast pinot noirs and our single-vineyard pinot noir, is loaded through hatches in the top of the cylinder into the slightly smaller presses, sophisticated microchip-governed devices that use a soft membrane driven horizontally to squeeze the juice into a large tray below. This tray is on casters of its own and has a drainage device attached to another food-grade hose, which leads to the same storage tank one level below. This juice is called the press wine and it amalgamates with the free-run wine in the holding tank.

Because there are no grunting workers turning a massive screw, it's hard to see how strongly the membrane presses the pomace. The correct procedure is "light and slow." Few winemakers now press too hard, on the theory that the press wine would become too tannic and astringent. Jensen agrees.

What happens to the pomace afterwards? On the farms where I grew up, the pressing would be even lighter than the modern practice. Then, in violation of all winemaking sense, the press residue or pomace would be dumped into a clean tank, topped up with water, sugar and acid and a yeast culture added, and another batch of "wine" (which even these parsimonious farmers called "false wine") would be made. This was given to the workers later in lieu of reasonable wages. It was pretty dismaying stuff. Calera, in common with other wineries, dumps the pomace. Elsewhere, it's occasionally used as fertilizer on the vineyards.

From this point on, as Steve Doerner used to put it, "It's real dirty winemaking. Mix it all together and stick it in barrel."

Our Jensen 1990 free-run wine and press wine sat in the storage tank for only a few hours, just long enough to settle the grossest of the "gross lees," the sludgy sediment substantially made up of dead yeast cells. After that, they went into barrels as unfiltered, untreated, new red wine.

The Davis red wine "recipe" would more typically leave the new wine in its tank for a week to settle the gross lees, and then filter and treat it, perhaps centrifuge it to clear it further and only then put it into barrels, almost clear, but utterly without character, the enological equivalent of canned peas.

Josh Jensen, however, subscribes to the old-school Burgundian belief that at least some of the gross lees in the barrel will add body and dimension to the wine. "This is an absolutely horrifying concept to the sanitation-is-everything school of winemaking from UC Davis," he said, after the by-now-obligatory "I don't want to be a Davis-basher, but ..." He believes strongly that one reason the heartbreak grape is breaking fewer hearts is that Oregon and California producers of pinot noir are of like mind on many issues such as this one. "What distinguishes the good new days from the bad old days is that many of us went back to the source, to Burgundy. We'd ask, 'Well, how do they do it? How is the stuff supposed to be made?' We weren't satisfied just saying, 'Oh yeah, it's a red wine, I know how to make red wine ...'"

After five hours in the holding tank, our Jensen 1990 flowed through more hose to the level below, where the crew was waiting with newly cleaned barrels. Steve Doerner, who was then still Calera's winemaker, was waiting with clipboard and pencil and directions; each batch (the Early, the Middle and the Late) and each vineyard block had been fermented separately and would be barreled and labeled as such. For the white wines, the barrels would be filled only five-sixths, to allow room for continuing fermentation. The pinot noir barrels were filled almost to the top, the bungs inserted, the "labels"—small pieces of paper with identifiers scrawled on them ("10/25/90 Jensen Early")— stapled to the barrel fronts and the barrels then stacked in long rows, five tiers high, each barrel separated by small wooden chocks.

Building the stacks, as arranging these serried ranks of barrels is called, is not as easy as it looks. Jensen, having tried it himself, is full of admiration for his cellar foreman, Abraham Corona. "The man's a near genius at lining up those barrels, five rows high, straight as an arrow, all by eye. In the days when I used to do it my stacks never looked like Abraham's. Most people who do this use ten-foot-long levels; Sara bought one for Abraham but he just put it in the corner and it's still there."

Our bottle-to-be stayed in its barrel for the next fifteen months. But it wasn't—entirely—left alone.

This matter of the barrels is not as simple as you might think. Why barrels? Why this size? Why oak? Why, in particular, French oak?

Premium wines, and wines capable of aging for the long term, are almost always aged in barrel, usually fifty- or sixty-gallon oak barrels. Many premium white wines are also fermented in barrel, which seems to produce a wine with more depth, more dimensions to it, than those from stainless-steel tanks; perhaps, as the wine breathes in air through the wood, it takes on some of the aromas of the cellar.

Why sixty gallons seems the correct size, no one really knows. Perhaps it was trial and error over the centuries. Perhaps it was just a manageable size to stack. Perhaps that's how big the oak trees grew in the forests of Allier in central France. Perhaps, as Jensen suspects, a sixty-gallon barrel imparts just the correct amount of flavor from the oak into the wine. Trial and error have shown that such a barrel seems to allow just enough oxygen to the right amount of wine to affect flavor positively, subtly and beneficially, softening the acids and tannins in the wine. Wine under gas in a stainless-steel tank will grow or develop only minimally, changing little over the years. Another advantage is the relatively short distance (about two and a half feet) the sediment has to drop before the wine is clear. "Whatever the reason, sixty gallons seems to work. I don't know why. Maybe someone will find an eighty-three-gallon size that works even better, or thirty-one gallons, but sixty is what the French have used for centuries. It's part of my method. Let's at least start with what the Burgundians do and then branch off if we find something better. If it ain't broke in Burgundy, then don't fix it here. But if it is broke, if there's something you can do to make better wine, then start doing that."

Our Jensen 1990 would spend its fifteen months in French oak barrels made to careful specification by a specific cooper in France who makes his barrels in a particular way out of wood from a designated forest. About a third of the wine will sit in barrels that are new. None of it will be in barrels more than six years old. The new barrels will impart a warm and exotically perfumed flavor to the finished wine, a heady mix of vanilla, spices and a buttery richness.

Oak barrels are one of the reasons premium wines cost premium prices.

Calera's barrels are a mix of woods from the central French oak forests of Allier, Tronçais, Limousin and Nevers. But Josh Jensen doesn't get into what he calls "hairsplitting" on this matter of barrels. At least, not much: "We just buy what we believe to be the best barrels, from a cooper with an impeccable reputation. It's very important that it be French oak, not American. Medium toast."

Not American oak? Medium toast? This is not hairsplitting?

For producers with a finely tuned nose and a passionate demand for precision and nuance, it's really not. Many American winemakers are considerably fussier than Jensen, specifying even the thickness of the staves and the style of the hoops. And this business of French oak is not just Old-World chauvinism: oak with a tight grain will release its desirable flavors more gradually. In general, oak from poor soil away from rivers is best—which is why the Nevers, Tronçais, Limousin and Allier forests are so much in demand. Other French forests produce a looser grain, too strong for wine. American oaks are also loose-grained and give wines a creamy taste, but are regarded as too strongly flavored.

Jensen feels that American oak can be fine for some varieties, like zinfandel or cabernet sauvignon, but not for pinot noir or chardonnay. "Too bad, too—we could save a lot of money if we didn't have to buy new French barrels every year. But the smell and taste of American oak is somehow out of place with chardonnay or pinot noir. The combination of pinot noir—and chardonnay—with French oak is absolutely wonderful—one of the perfect harmonies."

Still, if producers are not nitpickers, French coopers are hedged around with so much tradition as to seem positively fusty. The trees, for example, are split by hand along the grain, never sawn (so that the coarser oils are not released into the wine); the wood is then weather-dried (never, horrors, in a kiln) for somewhere between three and seven years. Then it's cut by hand into the thirty staves that will make up one barrel.

Only about twenty percent of an oak tree is suitable for staves and a hundred-year-old tree may only yield enough wood for a handful of barrels.

The staves are bent into the barrel shape over a fire of oak chips and shavings—the coopers never use steam heat or gas. It takes at least forty minutes to do the job and it needs precise handling not to let the fire become so hot that it chars the wood. Gradually the cellulose fibers in the wood break down and the vanillins and aromatics are fused into a kind of sweet caramel, glistening gray like the coat of a silver fox. It smells of new wood and bananas and cream, and every other kind of childish delight. This caramel, which will dissolve over a year or so into the wine the barrel will eventually contain, is described by winemakers as "toast." Winemakers can order their barrels with high, medium or low toast. Calera prefers medium.

Most of the barrels in which the Jensen '90 were aged were made in France by the largest family-owned cooperage in the world, François Frères of St.-Romain. The head of the firm, Jean François, spends much of his life in the forests searching for appropriate trees and seasons the wood in the meadows above St.-Romain. The firm produces only about seventy-five barrels a day; his clients include the Domaine de la Romanée-Conti, the Hospices de Beaune, Henri Jayer and Domaine A. Rousseau.

A few of the Calera barrels, however, were made by another cooper, which Josh Jensen refers to as D&J, shorthand for Dargaud et Jaeglé. He wasn't impressed and is unlikely to buy them again. "The D&J—I had never really carefully tasted them before but they taste resiny to me, they taste like D&J doesn't do enough air-drying of staves."

Each barrel costs better than six hundred dollars and Calera has about a thousand, Jensen calculates. "We get about twenty-four, twenty-five cases to the barrel and we'll make about twenty-five thousand cases this year, so that means we have about a thousand barrels. We order about a hundred and twenty brand-new barrels every year and sell them six to ten years later. This is a little like selling off a Cadillac after going round the block a couple of times, but it's the price of going first class."

❊   ❊   ❊

If at this point Jensen and his winemaker did nothing further, several things might happen to the wine. It could gradually age and mature, as the polymers in the wine grew longer and more complex chains; if there was an iota of sugar remaining, the yeast cells could finish their work, giving off a final trace of carbon dioxide; any contact with oxygen could irrevocably spoil the wine; the batch might—or might not—undergo a secondary, bacterial, malolactic fermentation; or it would do none of these things, which would be the worst outcome of all, since it would run the risk of undergoing its malolactic fermentation in bottle, either popping the corks in the wine shop (leading the wine merchant to demand his money back) or tasting putrid and looking cloudy to the consumer, which would make a lot of wine drinkers very cross and put the winemaker out of business if it happened very often.

The winemaker has to intervene at this point, if only to make sure the wine is microbiologically stable.

Under the Davis recipe, the solution seemed simple and obvious: stabilize the wines with relatively massive doses of sulfur dioxide and sterile filter it thoroughly through a mesh only a few microns wide, to rid the wine of any further 'hazards.' This worked. Of course, it also removed much of the flavor and complexity, the life of the wine.

The presence of sugar or of natural malic acid in any wine renders it susceptible to further fermentation, since it has not yet achieved microbiological stability. Winemakers typically view such wines as time bombs just waiting to explode. Such "explosions" would obviously alienate the customers and leave metaphoric egg on their professional reputations. The secondary or malolactic fermentation can occur spontaneously—in Europe, folklore says it's generated by some mysterious natural harmony, and starts with the rising of the sap in the vineyard. In more prosaic reality, it's the action of a bacterium, the leucanostoc, that metabolizes malic acid and converts it to the softer, and stable, lactic acid.

Calera not only doesn't try to prevent this malolactic fermentation, but actively encourages it. They want it. No, they demand it, and leave nothing to chance: they inoculate each batch with a bacterial culture that initiates it.

The reason Davis historically discouraged malolactic fermentation is because it's high-risk winemaking: to allow the leucanostoc to do its work, the wine must have little or no protective sulfur in it—leucanostoc is very intolerant of sulfur—and must be kept warmer than you'd normally store wines. It's high-risk because these same two conditions, low sulfur and high temperature, are also ideal for vinegar bacteria and other nasty critters. Even if the wines don't "spoil," they're susceptible under those conditions to simple oxidation. So you must encourage a swift secondary fermentation, and bite your nails in the meantime.

I'd noticed, on a shelf above the tangle of Bunsen burners and test tubes in Steiner's small lab, a plastic tub that looked something like a large margarine container, and asked her what it was. "Oh," she said airily, "it's a bacterial culture I'm keeping warm."

Some wineries, she told me, have isolated their own strain of bacterium. She purchases a number of different strains from a supply house in Sonoma, each one known for a different property. "You just grow batches of it and transfer that to the wine."

Yes, but how much do you add?

"A small amount, a cup, maybe two hundred millilitres, into each barrel. Maybe ... We want to see a nice steady metabolism of the malic acid, but how much you need for, say, a sixty-gallon barrel is not so simple a question. How many chains of bacteria do you need to do the job? Nobody really has an answer, it's hard to say. It's not nearly as simple a process as the primary fermentation. I can have all kinds of cultures in buckets and they're growing beautifully, there are tons of chains of bacteria, but put it in a barrel and it just stops. I've taken to adding a small amount of nutrient to the wine to get them going. This is really a source of nitrogen for the yeasts that remain. Yeasts are very aggressive; they eat up all the nutrients and there's nothing left for the bacteria. So ... feed the yeast and they'll leave something for the bacteria.

"You've got to go with what's tried and true and what works. There are good years and bad years, and different nutrient levels in the grapes. At Calera every barrel is its own little entity. The malolactic might happen anyway; I'm just reassuring myself that the ingredients for the malolactic are in place."

I asked Jensen why the malolactic fermentation was so important. He believes it's "absolutely a key to making great pinot noirs, as it is, in my opinion, a key to making great chardonnays. Malolactic fermentation for pinot noir and other reds was accepted earlier in this country than it was for the chardonnays. Even now, the majority of chardonnays, even in the twelve dollar and up category, are not malolactic chardonnays. For it's somewhat high risk, and the advantages of the chardonnay having gone through the malolactic are not universally recognized."

What does it do to the wine?

"At least three distinct things. First, it lowers the total acidity of the wine. This is neither good nor bad, just a fact. Malic acid is stronger than the lactic acid the wine ends up with, so the total acidity will always go down a bit.

"A second thing it does is add complexity to the wine. People often describe it as a buttery character, particularly in chardonnay. It adds an extra dimension, an extra subtlety to the wine and in my opinion, what separates the great pinot noirs in the world, whether they are made in France, here or in Oregon or New Zealand, from the everyday run-of-the-mill ones is complexity. Not brute force, not powerhouse flavors, not silky smooth elegance, it's complexity—different layers of smell and taste. The malolactic, for a pinot noir, is essential if you are going to get all the complexity in that wine of which it's capable.

"And then finally the malolactic fermentation renders the wine microbiologically stable, therefore you don't have to filter it, which would take out much of the good along with the bad.

"So it's absolutely the key to making the wines in the philosophy that we want to make them, because if you can't get them to go through malolactic fermentation, you must sterile filter. And then you get the second-rate."

As soon as the malolactic fermentation is over, the wine is given a very small dose of sulfur dioxide, usually only eighty parts per million, which in this case acts as an anti-oxidant and bactericide.

To know when to do that is not so simple a matter either. Steiner uses an instrument called a spectrophotometer and runs a series of enzymatic analyses to see how much, if any, malic acid is left in the wine. "You do that for every barrel. There must be a thousand barrels but I don't want to count. " She laughed. "So I start with composites, batches, and work backwards if I find malic acid still present. We're looking for diminishing malic acid. You don't really care about the lactic. Presence of lactic isn't the issue. What you want is to eliminate the malic, get it so low that the wine is microbiologically stable. If you don't filter and you put the wine in the bottle, there's not enough malic acid in there for any residual bacteria to create any fermenting problems in your bottle."

I told Jensen that this all sounded suspiciously chemical to me, but he was indignant. "Not at all," he said. "We're protecting a perfectly natural process. We're just doing what we do all along, which is to shape events so the natural process can happen uneventfully." Later, he poured me a glass of his chardonnay and demanded I dip my nose into it. Obediently, I did so. "Take a small sip," he instructed, "and let it sit a moment on the palate." I did this too. "See!" he said triumphantly. "Is the difference not clear?"

The wine sat on the back of my tongue, smooth as glycerin. I let the aroma drift up into my nostrils. It was true—underlying the fruit was a faint, faint flavor of fresh farm butter, overlaid with a hint of vanilla. I thought for some reason of my grandmother, perhaps because she used vanilla in her baking, and caught a quick mental snapshot of her arms, ropy with hard usage, up to the elbows in a tub of butter and flour, and I could smell the warm dairy acids from the barn behind the farmhouse. I admitted that if it were the lactic acid I was tasting, it was a thing to be admired. "See!" he said again, and pressed the cork back into the bottle, slapping it into place. "It's one more thing that makes better wines better."

XIV

*In which our wine makes its way from
barrel to bottle, and in which the
techniques of racking and fining
are discussed and dismissed*

For the next twelve to fourteen months, the winemakers are essentially babysitting. Very little more is done to the wine except periodic topping up of the barrels to compensate for evaporation losses, and constant monitoring by the taste panel of Jensen, Steiner and Vita to see that nothing untoward was happening.

The wine is not "racked" at all in this period.

This is another departure from standard practice. Racking is a simple method of getting rid of the dead yeast and other sediment. The "clean" wine, wine in which sediment has largely settled, is gently pumped or siphoned off the sediment or "lees" into a new barrel. The sediment is then thrown away and the original barrel cleaned and readied for re-use. Virtually all red wines are racked and not just by Davis rules: it's a natural way of protecting and beneficially aerating the wine. Unracked wines run a greater risk of spoilage, a risk, as Jensen puts it, that "some unwanted character and smells will creep into the wine from the sediment, from the dead yeast."

So why does he resist racking?

"Well," he says, "I can understand why it drives the professors to distraction. They look at that thick sludge in the barrel and they say, 'God, it's so dirty ... you can't do that, it's backwards winemaking.'" But racking does something else to wine too: it diminishes color, body and flavor. And since pinot noir is the "especially grape," racking especially takes away color, body and flavor from pinot noir wines. "If your goal is to make merely sound but boring wines, then the professors are right. Not racking *is* risky. But if you're aiming to compete at the highest levels and to get the wine into the bottle at its ultimate potential, you need to take those risks, because the wine can't afford to give up any color, any flavor, any body or complexity."

In Calera's early years, the vintages of '78, '79 and '80, Josh Jensen did three or four rackings through the production cycle. He stopped on the advice of Aubert de Villaine, who visited Calera in the early winter of '81, tasted the '81 vintage and asked what had been done to it. He suggested less racking.

"We experimented immediately—half the current batch was racked, half not, and we consistently preferred the unracked wines. They had more color and flavor and guts, more middle." With the '82s, Calera converted to a no-racking regimen. "And that's more or less where we are today. We belong to a technical group called the Small Winery Technical Society, with a lot of the pinot noir specialists as members, and in comparing notes, most of us have abandoned racking. Interestingly, Romanée-Conti these days doesn't even do the two rackings we still do, into the fining tank and into the bottling tank. They don't fine, clarify, at all, but bottle directly from each barrel, barrel by barrel. Since they pick each vineyard in one pass they don't have to recombine the wine, and since they use only new barrels, they can get away with it.

"We can't, because we age our wines in a mixture of new and older barrels. For us, bottling straight from the barrel would result in some bottles—those from new barrels—being much oakier, and in my opinion too much oakier, than the bottles from the older barrels. It's important that each wine batch be uniform. So we appear to be locked in to doing the minimum of two rackings, right before bottling.

"Also, in tasting our wines, I seem to prefer the flavor of wine that's been lightly fined with egg whites. It gives it a little bit of elegance and it certainly does make the wine clearer. If the time comes when we do fining trials of one vintage and we find that we like it better unfined and don't want to fine it, we won't do it."

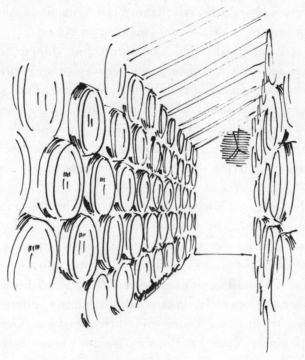

By January 1 the tempo of cellar samplings starts to pick up. Each fermentation tank batch (there is usually at least an Early, Middle and Late batch of each wine) has spent better than a year in barrels as a separate wine batch. The winemakers do endless samplings, assembling composites or prototypes of the wines-to-be, tasting and retasting the prototypes. They go through several "every-barrel tastings" to see if they like the way the wine is taking shape. They check and recheck the sulfur dioxide levels. Some barrels may need a small dose of sulfur to help keep them fresh. The winemaker takes notes; the cellar workers, using her clipboard, move through the cellars adding the sulfur.

"What we're tasting for," Steiner told me (adopting the didactic tone of her employer), "is development. We're looking for the maturation, the chemical change of the wine. We're looking for anything funny, anything off, that might be happening in the barrel. You might find something like that occasionally. On the other hand, you might find a batch or a series of barrels that are just dynamite, really exceptional development. Those are ones you keep an eye on."

She became animated. "Wines do interesting things. Some, for example, may age really quickly in a positive way—they're precocious. Others tend to be tight and it takes them a long time. This is my first year here, and these are the kinds of things I'm looking for, looking to learn. I need to get to know the personalities of the wines. What is this vineyard like, what does that block do and how typical is this?"

In Josh Jensen's terms, she was making friends with the wine.

Finally, when the composite seems ready for bottling, and after Jensen, Steiner and Vita have gone through the exercise of tasting and evaluating the prototypes several times, the batches are amalgamated or assembled or "put together," each one into its own tank. Jensen is fussy about the terminology here. He won't use the word "blending" for this operation because that connotes different grape varieties together in a single wine—anathema to the serious-minded pinot noir producer. Calera isn't mixing varieties here—each wine is a hundred percent pinot noir—and each prototype comes entirely from one individual vineyard.

These amalgams make considerably more complex wines than any of the single batches. The amalgams allow the Calera crew to sift through the batches, choosing a base, a backbone, a fruit, a structure, the nose, the finish. "Josh will say, and it's true, that when you put the parts together you really do get something better than any one individual. I think the most exciting thing about a wine is what you can call complexity, and that tends to be lacking a lot of times in a lot of wines, and this is one way to get complexity, this careful control of the composites."

I asked Jensen at one point whether he'd ever thought of blending pinot noir with another grape, in whatever percentage? He looked horrified. "No. Absolutely not. Don't ever blend pinot noir. Not even one percent."

By early May 1992, after fifteen months in barrel, our Jensen 1990 was almost ready for bottle. The composites had been tested and pronounced good. There were no bad barrels. The samples drawn by the thief were clear, though not yet brilliant. The wine still needed to be fined—the last of its sedimentary particles removed.

Not, however, through the Davis techniques of centrifuging (which would remove flavor as well as impurities), ion exchange, cold stabilization or filtration. Not for the reds.

Josh does, on the other hand, lightly filter his white wines. He's unapologetic about this apparent double standard. "Whites are more fragile, they need more temperature control, they need filtration, at least the very light filtration we employ. We never even owned a filter until we started making chardonnay, and we still only have a little teeny plate-and-frame filter and a small lees filter. Wines with residual sugar or malic acid have to be sterile filtered—by sterile I mean you take everything out, including a lot of the flavor—but our wines, even our whites, have no sugar or malic acid in them, so we can do a very light filtration. We could bottle them without filtration, and there are some wineries that do, but I like the taste of our wines better when they've been lightly filtered. We do it to our taste. We'll do a lab trial with two or three different levels of filterings and pick the one that tastes best."

But the pinot noirs—never.

Or at least—not so far.

There's one condition that would demand filtration. Occasional vintages, in Burgundy and elsewhere, just won't clear by themselves, even with the help of fining agents, and have to be filtered. Although Jensen is braced for it to happen at Calera, he has yet to face it. No one knows why it happens, although winemaking lore is full of theories, including an old injunction to rack only on the waxing of the moon, which may or may not have something to do with air pressure and almost certainly has a lot to do with a kind of cheerfully gloomy superstition. "If we ever find ourselves in that situation we may need to do a very light filtration, as light as possible, but we haven't yet, thank God."

White wines have to be more meticulously fined than reds to achieve that happy state called "protein stability"—without which the whites would turn cloudy when refrigerated, discombobulating the consumer and disconcerting the winery's cash flow. In Calera's case they're fined by dropping a cloud of fine clay called Bentonite through the wine. The clay drags the sediment down with it as it sinks to the bottom.

Red wines are fined very gently. Calera uses the traditional Burgundian method, involving egg whites. These are vigorously stirred into the wine. Since the egg whites carry a positive electrical charge, they attract suspended colloidal particles, which are negatively charged, to form large molecules that are heavy enough to drop fairly rapidly through the liquid. The stirring has to be done with some dispatch because the electrical charge disappears within a few minutes, and it's not as easy as it might sound—giving six hundred gallons of liquid a vigorous stirring isn't as simple as stirring a sugar cube into a cup of tea. Six hundred gallons is *heavy*.

The number of egg whites that are necessary varies from year to year and batch to batch, depending on the particulate matter suspended in the wine. Sara Steiner will conduct lab trials to find the minimum number that will do the trick—it can range from a low of one per sixty gallons to six. Our 1990s took five.

All the Jensen 1990s were, finally, consolidated in one stainless-steel tank—all three pickings and the two additional batches from separate blocks within the vineyard. The wine sat on its finings for seventeen days and the clear wine was then carefully drawn off the top and put into the bottling tank.

And so to bottle.

It was June 19, 1992.

XV

*In which the subtle matter of
quality is discussed, and the
even more elusive matters of hype,
propaganda and fashion*

So there it sits, our bottle of

> CALERA
> JENSEN
> MT. HARLAN
> PINOT NOIR
> 1990,

along with about eleven thousand of its fellows, boxed and loaded
onto pallets, carefully stacked to one side of a yellow line painted on
the floor of the lowest level of the winery (that's the arbitrary line
imagined into being by the tax-happy federal bureaucrats; once the
wine crosses that line it is deemed to have left the winery and is
immediately subject to tax, whether or not it has been sold). Those
cases of wine will wait there, storage space willing, until they are
deemed old enough to go out into the world on their own.

It is now finished wine, no longer grape juice.

Still a young thing, callow, not yet ready for a serious relationship
with a real drinker.

Is it any good?

Will it get any better?

And who says so?

There are three or four ways of looking at it: the chemist's way, the connoisseur's way, the marketer's way and the drinker's way. All of these intersect.

From the chemist's point of view, the wine is a complex liquid the value of which is basically water plus a synthesis of chemical flavors from the juice, skin, pulp and seeds of the grape, containing numerous compounds and elements, including: residual sugar (usually less than 0.2 percent of non-fermentable pentose sugars, such as xylose, ribose and arabinose; the glucose and fructose, the fermentable sugars, have been metabolized by the yeasts); fixed acids such as malic (the predominant acid in apples), lactic and tartaric; various volatile acids; isoamyl alcohols; pigments (chemists support Josh's notion that pinot noir is shy on color; under analysis through chromatography, nine pigments can be detected in cabernet, eight in zinfandel but only four in pinot noir); considerable numbers of subtle phenolic compounds, classes of "flavoids" that determine the minute differences between individual wines; trace minerals; and tannins.

Traditional winemakers understand the utility of these chemical histograms of wine and, despite their inherent distrust of the laboratory, generally approve of anything that enables them to understand their product better. They know—or believe—that chemists will never be able to make great wines in the lab, but it's reassuring to know that great wines actually exist, and not just in the minds of their makers or of the industry propagandists. It's also reassuring to know why something happens. For example, if you know that the phenolic compounds in the wine link together over time to form longer polymers, you'll more easily understand why a wine tastes and smells different when it gets older. In young wines there's an unresolved blend of acids, sugars, minerals, pigments, esters, aldehydes and tannins. It takes time for these elements to resolve themselves into a complex but congruent whole. When the polymers get too long, they drop out of suspension and the wine begins to deteriorate.

At the same time, the chemists don't know everything. While they're beginning to be able to build a three-dimensional schematic of a typical "great wine," there's still so much variation, and so many reasons for the variations, that the practical utility of such knowledge is limited. Winemakers still have to trust their intuition and experience; farmers still make better wines than chemists.

And these farmers still take things ... personally. Josh Jensen tells a story he once heard in Bordeaux, at a winemaking seminar, that neatly illustrates the philosophical differences.

The story tells of the proprietor of a large, well-financed Bordeaux château (for the purposes of the story, always unnamed). He was very wealthy and all his equipment was first class. There was no better-equipped winery in all of France. All his senior executives drove Mercedes as they tooled down to the shippers to send their wines abroad. But the property never made wines that won wine competitions or were fêted at the annual dinners of wine connoisseurs.

One day the proprietor instructed his managers to visit his neighbor, a farmer who had little money and whose winery was, to put it politely, rustic. On the other hand, his wines always received better ratings from wine lovers and won competitions.

"I want you to learn exactly how he makes his wines, so we can do it here," they were instructed. "With our superior equipment, we'll then turn out wines that are better than his."

The string of Mercedes duly set off and were greeted at the neighboring château with politeness. The farmer was a simple man, but he understood perfectly what they wanted.

"Well," he said, "let me first ask you one question."

"Okay," they said, "what is it?"

And he asked, "Do you love your wines?"

What?

"Do you love your wines?" he asked again.

Since they didn't know how to answer the question, they got back into their Mercedes and returned to their own winery.

"Well, what did you learn?" their proprietor asked.

"Nothing," they said. "He made no sense. He doesn't have any secrets. There's nothing to learn."

Josh Jensen tells the story with relish, in the vocabulary and rhythms of a parable. To him it contains a very large truth about wine. He's a man who really does love his wines. They are not just inanimate objects, numbers on a chart, figures for the bottom line, a calculus of cash. He loves them in a parental way; he worries that they're going to be all right; late at night, when the others have gone home, he'll sometimes get up and walk through the winery, laying a hand against the cool barrels, breathing in the heady, clean, fruity aroma of the cellars. In the burning months of the California summer he'll go down to the cellars late at night and open the doors, turning on the fans to let the cool air caress the waiting wine.

Maynard Amerine, the eminent emeritus professor at Davis, the person who wrote or co-authored most of the standard English-language wine textbooks, told Josh, when he was starting out, to be wary of losing the scientifically detached air of the technician. Never talk about the personality, or the mood, of wine, the great man said, and since Josh was a young man and just starting, he took the advice to heart. Or he tried to, but it was no use. He did treat his wines with love and with wonder; he does, in that ugly anthropological word, anthropomorphize them; he does regard them as live beings.

He'll wonder about their mood, the mood of a certain batch of wine, or a barrel or two that doesn't seem up to par, or a batch that seems anxious and forward. Sometimes a batch, for no apparent reason, will get cranky, or weary, or will withhold its charms, or be shy. These are all terms Josh uses and all phases he can recognize in his wines.

At the large winery level, where wines are manufactured as much as made, Professor Amerine's advice was probably sound. But Josh believes that believing in their personalities helps make it true—it's a part of why great wine does indeed have recognizable characteristics.

He soon discovered that no matter how much attention he gave each batch and each barrel, some always turned out better than others, and like any parent, it worried and delighted him. "Sure," he says, "it gives you sleepless nights. You worry more, whether you should do something to a wine, or withhold something. If you're emotionally involved it matters more, and decisions on when to pick, when to inoculate with the malolactic bug, when to bottle, become more personal. They are almost like your children, and if you have three barrels of wine that, because of the type of high-risk winemaking I feel we have to do, irrevocably spoil, turn to complete vinegar and we have to dump 'em down the drain or sell them to a distillery for a few cents a gallon, well, I mourn them, I feel sick. You can say, 'Well, you've got a thousand barrels after all,' but that's like saying, 'Well, you shouldn't worry if only three of your children die because you've got others.' I do worry and I take it hard. It's unrelated to the dollar loss. There is a dollar loss, yes, but I'm not emotional about that. I don't like it, it ticks me off, yes, but I'm not sick to death over it. I'm sick over the fact that those three barrels died."

What is the personality of our bottle of Jensen 1990, still sitting on its pallets? He had surely tasted enough of them to get a sense of how they were.

He was, for Josh, uncharacteristically reticent to pronounce judgment on his wines. Partly, he confesses, out of laziness and partly out of a belief that his job was to make the stuff and it was the job of the critics and consumers to judge them. There's also a sense that categoric judgments get in the way of enjoyment; it's a truism in the wine business that in the matter of taste everyone is right (with the accompanying suspicion that the wine writers' and critics' pronouncements are largely hyperbole and, by giving the matter of tasting wine an air of profundity through the use of arcane language, they actually interfere with the enjoyment of wine by perfectly sensible and ordinary people). At first, he referred me to the descriptions in Oz Clarke's book *The New Classic Wines*, in which Clarke described his single-vineyard wines this way: "Jensen is the most open, with deliciously accessible flavors of strawberry and honey, sometimes developing an almost candied sweetness which ages to a thrilling combination of raspberry sauce richness, swished with the rasping perfume of leather. Reed has a less dense style—combining the savory perfumes of roast coffee and earth with a fruit of blackberry and the herbal aromas of sassafras. Selleck is denser in every way. More tannic, slower to evolve, but magnificently perfumed, full of the classic Burgundian entangled mysteries of cherry and plum, wild raspberry, toast and cinnamon spice. The vines of the Mills vineyard were only planted in 1984, but already the wines are exhibiting that rarest and most haunting of perfumes—that of violets.

"What Calera needs is to get some stability of crop so that a true style can emerge. The 1988s, for instance, born out of severe drought conditions yielding less than half a ton per acre, are magnificent, yet almost grotesque, still young, still packed with the dense flavors of youth and yet possessing a core so deep and old they seem like children grown old before they were ever young. The 1989s, with twice the crop, lose nothing in beauty, but gain enormously in freshness and balance. 1987 had the biggest crop so far, yet many critics hail 1987 Selleck as the finest yet."

I pushed Josh for his own version of this.

"Okay," he said, "but first let me say that I can't always pick them out in tastings, not even whether it's a Calera wine or not. I've tasted our wines at the Vintner's Club in San Francisco, and in recent years I find that if I like one wine more than the others it will turn out to be a Calera. In early years I'd go into the tasting looking for our wine, instead of just concentrating on the wines at hand, and it would get me all screwed up, so in the end I'd neither find our wine nor achieve a cogent analysis of the wines there."

He stopped, shook his head. "When I first started, I went to an important tasting at the top of the Bank of America building put on by *Connoisseurs Guide to California Wine*. This was in the formative years of California pinot noir, and the '79 Selleck, a very fine wine of ours, was in it. The results were to be reported in their publication, which was quite important at that time. When I taste wines I can have great days when I'm perceptive and accurate, and days when I'm off the mark. I know, as soon as I get into a tasting, what kind of day it will be. That day, I had one of those bad days. I ranked our '79 Selleck last. If I'd not been at that tasting, the '79 Selleck would have won and put us on the map. Instead, it came in third because of my twelfth-place vote. I'll carry that guilt with me until my grave. It took us four more years to get to the top of the heap.

"After a while I learned to relax and resolved just to go in and find which wine I liked the best, which the worst and which in between, and rank them, and since I started doing that, more often than not, I prefer ours.

"So, I don't think there's an attribute to each of the four vineyards that will categorically identify each one. We go to great lengths when we're picking to bring each vineyard in at the same average ripeness and to age them in the exact same percentage of brand new barrels. We try to treat each vineyard's wine equally, so the consumer will never be able to say that a wine 'must be' a Reed, say, because it has less ripe flavors.

"The Mills still seems to me to have the character of a young vineyard. Sara identified that at the end of our most recent tasting. She said it seemed tannic, and asked whether it was a characteristic of that vineyard. I said it was a characteristic of young vines. Young vines give a certain skeleton or structure to a wine, and when they get older, the hope is that more fleshiness and fatness, the middle flavors and palette, will come into the wine. So the Mills has this terrific structure but it often seems leaner than the other three. The Mills vines are nine years younger. Compared to any other pinot noir from other American producers it is rich, full flavored, dark and complex. But compared to our own vineyards it seems less rounded and supple and fat by comparison.

"The Reed most years has to me a sort of chocolatey, raisiny character. In personality it has acquired a softness and precociousness. It seems to get ready and say 'Drink me' before the others do. It almost always has the lightest color. I've sometimes seen a lighter brick color right out of the press, although this is usually a sign of some age in a wine. Partly for that reason we now release it first of the four single-vineyard wines. It's very smooth. Of course, the whole process of barrel aging of wine is one of smoothing and softening the wine, and that process continues in the bottle, but much more slowly. The trick in bottling is to capture the wine just at the perfect moment where it is still crisp but really lush.

"The Selleck is my personal favorite almost every vintage. As the Reed is the fastest to evolve, the Selleck is the slowest. For some reason, and we don't know why, it's always the Selleck that's the last to get clear in the barrels, the last to taste like wine in the barrels, the last to show its true quality and the last to come out of "bottle shock" after it's been bottled. It seems to have one more layer, one more bit of depth and complexity than the others, and since complexity is what I appreciate the most it appeals to me the most. The Selleck is the most feminine of our wines, the most subtle. It seems to taste spicy, nutmeg, truffles and earth together, floral, so it is complete and complex. Not in every vintage. The '90 Selleck I don't think is going to be the best wine of the vintage. The '88 Selleck is so rock-like it's hard to know if it's going to be the best from that vintage. The '89 I think will be. In '82 it was, and in '84 it was, though the '84 Jensen was awfully close to it. In 1990 the Jensen is the standout."

I nodded. Good! I'd become quite proprietary about the 1990 Jensen.

"The Jensen is the demand item of all of them and we price it accordingly, along with the Selleck, a notch above the other two. People ask for the Jensen because it's the biggest of the original vineyards and therefore many more bottles have gone out into the world, so people know it better. And although it's actually named after my father, that is also my name and I'm the guy going around to New York and Houston and Chicago talking about the wines ... 'Oh yes a Jensen, yeah that's the guy that came in here ...' It's the one restaurants always ask for.

"The Jensen is a complex wine and for me complexity—and consistency at being complex—is really the ultimate compliment to a pinot noir. Pinot noir doesn't want to allow you to be consistent. When people tell me our wines are good I'm complimented, but when they say they are consistent, that for me is the jackpot. Every winery in California has one great pinot noir in it and very often only one. To do it year after year, that's the challenge, the achievement. The Jensen is usually the most tannic and also the leanest, the least rounded. It has a sort of olive character, a spiciness, and ... well, the well runs dry. Ask Oz Clarke. Or Robert Parker.

"I think between five and twenty years is when our wines will be showing nicely. Sometimes wine writers who write about our estate pinot noirs say they are lighter-style wines to be drunk in a year or two. I think that's a misreading of these wines."

Like many people who drink wine for enjoyment rather than professional aggrandizement, I've always been put off by the rituals of wine tastings, with their arcane procedures and pretentious vocabulary; there's an inherent elitism in the world of fine wines that intimidates and drives away many a casual consumer. The world of the wine writer is one of magisterial authority; they have so much influence they begin to think they really matter, and they feel quite comfortable sneering at people who like a little residual sugar in their wines or who like to drink a blush wine with fried chicken.

There is, in fact, more disdain expressed for the ordinary consumer in the wine business than in any other subculture, with the possible exception of haute couture and the visual arts. After all, the differences between wines, particularly if they are fine wines of the same kind, are so small, so personal, so fleeting, a quick splash of sensation on the palate, that learning can quite interfere with enjoyment. You don't need a Ph.D. to appreciate wine; all you need is experience. The more you do it the better you get, and the experience is best gained drinking wine with food, for enjoyment, and not in the swirl-and-sniff environment of what are essentially trade shows.

Many tastings are snob tastings, but not all is foolishness and hype. There are some real reasons for what tasters do, for the sniffing and slurping and spitting that goes on at these affairs. It's governed, to some degree at least, by the physiology of taste. The tongue is a clumsy instrument; it can tell only whether the wine is sweet (at the tip) or sour (at the sides) or bitter (at the back). But

the real seat of flavor and aroma in the wine is the esters and aldehydes, which rise as vapor from behind the palate into the nasal cav-
ity. There they are dissolved and carried to the olfactory nerve center in the brain, and thence to the temporal lobe, where memory
resides. Memory is analyzed and judged in the higher lobes of the
brain. The alcohol in the wine facilitates this process but will also
very shortly upset the brain's equilibrium—which is why it is best
not to swallow if you're tasting a number of wines. Eighty percent of
the quality of the pleasure is in the smell and the nose, therefore, is
as important as the palate.

The consistency of expert reactions at blind tastings does indicate
that evaluating wine is not all illusion. Generally, experienced tasters
will agree on which wines are good and which are not. They might
have different rankings for numbers one and two, according to their
personal preferences, but they'll probably all agree on the top four.

The most difficult thing about tasting wine is describing it to others. The attributes are so elusive, and the standards for measuring
them so abstract, that writers must perforce fall back on fanciful
comparatives. (I thought back to the reading I'd done on pinot noir.
My favorite descriptor, from a wine writer I generally admire, was
"armpit," which she meant positively, if off-puttingly; and my favorite
winemaker's reaction came when a writer described his wine as
"smelling of eucalyptus" and he responded afterwards that he
thought "eucalyptus smelled of cat piss, but if they want to call it
eucalyptus and sell my wine for me, let them go ahead.") The more
common words used are butter, oak, toast, nuts, raspberries, citrus,
coffee, black tea, tar, truffles, peaches, vanilla, yeast, cigar box, earth
and our old friend eucalyptus. Wines are also described as spicy,
prickly, tannic, full-bodied, honeyed, raw, burnt, bitter, youthful,
closed, open, forward, reticent, alcoholic, mature, faded. There are
also a few useful descriptors that are more technical in their intent.
"Body," for example, means the heft of a wine and is attributed to its
alcoholic content; "finish" means the aftertaste—in great wine the flavor remains in the mouth for some time after tasting; "hard"
describes a particularly tannic wine that needs years, sometimes

decades, to mature; "supple" is its desirable opposite; "dumb" means wine not yet offering up its full quality and is similar to "closed," which can also mean something similar to hard.

Some time later, on my desk at home, I lined up bottles of Reed, Mills, Selleck and Jensen. I pulled the cork from the Jensen and poured a little into a clean glass, tilting it against a sheet of white paper on the desk. It was quite clear but not brilliantly so, with a deep ruby red color. I sniffed. There were, indeed, hints of strawberry and honey-vanilla, with a faint undertone of what I took to be a kind of old-leather aroma. In the mouth, the wine was still tight, a little astringent—it needed another couple of years—but the strawberries changed to raspberry jam. Try as I might, I detected no hint of violets, the one word everyone uses about the wines they love best.

I pushed the unopened wines aside—keeping the Jensen to hand to keep memory fresh—and riffled through a pile of clippings on the desk, reviews of Calera wines from the professionals, to see what they had to say. The first one I found I couldn't identify, the name of the writer and newspaper had disappeared from the clipping. Whoever it was said something I thought apt about Calera Central Coast pinot noir: "A fine wine, an intelligent wine—perfect pinot noir fruit, with the flavor of the limestone vineyards, with good structure, perfect harmony, nuance and surprise." Apt, but wrong: the Central Coast pinot noirs aren't made from grapes grown on Calera's own limestone vineyards.

There were many others:

California Grapevine said of the '87s that they were "medium to medium dark ruby color; initially somewhat subdued aroma which opened quickly to show very attractive, rich cherry fruit with spicy ripe currant overtones with a note of vanilla; medium full body; assertive and moderately concentrated fruit flavors on the palate; well structured and balanced; moderate tannin; lingering aftertaste. Superior quality and highly recommended."

Robert Parker's *Wine Advocate* liked Calera's Jensen the most— "The richest, darkest-colored, longest, most profound of Calera's offerings. It is also backward, very deeply concentrated, with multi-dimensional pinot noir flavors, and extraordinary presence and aromatic complexity." Wrote Parker: "Since 1984 Josh Jensen has been producing pinot noirs that approach the aromatic complexity and flavor dimension of the best French red burgundies, wines of extraordinary complexity that not only rival but also frequently surpass their French counterparts."

Joel Fleishman in *Vanity Fair* liked the Reed best: "Its nose of pungent, chewy black and red cherries leaps out of the glass, and in the mouth there's an explosion of clean, crisp, velvety black-cherry essences so rich and intense they make you gasp."

The judges at the International Wine challenge, in London in 1991, said the Jensen "impressed tasters with its deliciously ripe, raspberryish flavor."

Chewy cherries and currants, along with a little raspberry, seemed the fruits of choice. I began to wonder what had happened to grapes.

There were dozens of other clippings, from Frank Prial in *The New York Times*, Alexis Bespaloff in *New York* and many others — *Vines & Spirits*; *The Underground Wine Journal*; *The Wine Spectator*; *The Underground Wineletter*; *The Wall Street Journal*; Fleishman again; the *San Francisco Chronicle*; the *Connoisseurs Guide to California Wine*; the *Chicago Tribune*; *Wine Tidings* magazine (writer Tony Aspler liked the '83 Calera better than Chambolle-Musigny of the same year, and the Calera '82s better than the Romanée St. Vivant of that year); reports of the Vintners Club tastings of pinot noirs; the *Daily News*; *Wine Times* magazine; *Wine* magazine of London; *The New York Wine Cellar* ... They all liked Calera, and they all liked the Jensen. So did Oz Clarke, and most of the other new wine books.

Josh Jensen is wise enough to know that one of the reasons for his success as a winemaker has been because the wine critics like his wine; he understands the value of precise public relations — that an articulate tongue is as valuable to a winemaker as a fine palate. Influencing the influencers is important. In a country that is, still, wine-ignorant, if not hostile to wine, the people who write about wine are crucial; wine critics and the wine press are how retailers get to know what's going on, and a rave review can catapult a wine to the top. Many other makers of California pinot noirs produce first-rate wines too, but they've never been reviewed and their businesses are failing. Josh has warned his staff several times that there is no guarantee of continued coverage by the critics; they could decide on a whim to ignore Calera. "Maybe they'll decide we've had our fifteen minutes of fame," he says. "Maybe they'll think we're too big for our britches. I don't know. But we shouldn't expect this to go on."

There are a number of fine writers writing about wine—Frank Prial, Hugh Johnson, Alexis Bespaloff, Tony Aspler, Jancis Robinson, George Bain, James Chatto. But the two men with the greatest influence on the business in America are Robert Parker and Marvin Shanken.

Parker was a government lawyer from Maryland with a strictly local audience when he took two gambles that propelled him to the top of the critical heap. The first was to take an early and categoric stand on the contentious matter of the '82 Bordeaux vintage, about which the wine press had up till then been divided—was it the greatest of the century or were the wines overblown and overripe? Parker's public fight on this issue with the most-eminent-to-that-time wine writer, Robert Finigan, was a *succès de scandale* and propelled Parker to superstardom. Parker said the '82s were sublime, his view prevailed, the Bordeaux producers clasped him to their grateful bosoms and his newsletter, *The Wine Advocate*, became an instant critical success, as eagerly awaited and as feared as the *Guide Michelin* in the restaurant business. (It also reached twenty-one thousand subscribers, at thirty dollars each.) Finigan disappeared. Parker's second gamble was his adoption of Oregon as the future home of the world's best pinot noirs (and, a few years later, to enhance his reputation as a man who feared no vested interest, his magisterial denunciation of the very same Oregon producers he had lauded earlier). The third thing that gave him influence was his invention of the hundred-point scale for evaluating wines—the assigned number and the price made it easy for consumers to buy wines without having to wade through the admittedly overblown prose that accompanied his ratings. His invention is not without its detractors, although many others have now adopted it; some winemakers feel it creates an inappropriate atmosphere in which some wines win and some lose, and thereby lessens a broad appreciation for different wine styles.

In the course of an average week Parker will sip and spit his way through hundreds of bottles of wine (reds in the morning, whites in the afternoon). The judgments and ratings will make their way into his newsletter and, often, later be collected into a book. His judgments are always trenchant and frequently contrarian. A few years ago, when all of California and some British wine writers (including the great Hugh Johnson) were proclaiming (in Johnson's words) that "California challenges the world with ... a growing number of luxury wines of brilliant quality," Parker was writing: "Much of the self-serving, overly exaggerated publicity about the greatness of California wines ... is quite excessive and easily refutable ... California has much to learn."

Marvin Shanken was a former investment banker turned publishing entrepreneur. His magazine, *The Wine Spectator*, is the lifestyle magazine of the wine industry, filled with gossip and anecdote, personality profiles, hype. It also contains a serious buyers' guide and twice a year sponsors events called The Wine Experience, bi-coastal extravaganzas that bring together winemakers from America and Europe, critics and journalists, retailers and agents, and that have become an essential part of the wine calendar in America.

Many winemakers are skeptical, however, that the hype industry contributes very much to the health of the wine business. For one thing, by the nature of criticism, wine writers want to be taken seriously and therefore concentrate on the Big Wines. Generally, big means good, light means less good, serious means good, light and playful less good. These are not men of great good humor. They take much of the pure fun out of drinking wine. Finesse is not a word that has much meaning to them; ponderousness is the prevailing style. Josh Jensen believes that the hype, and the resulting dependence on fashion and opinion, is destructive in another way. "Fashion has a huge role in the American wine business. I deplore it. It creates a pendulum of demand, encouraged by *The Wine Spectator*. The magazine will do a cover, say, that says gewürztraminer is now "in" and we're all supposed to believe that's the variety of the year. Four or five years later they'll have a cover that says gewürztraminer is now dead, nobody is ever going to drink it again. I think this is so stupid. It's like declaring bread out of fashion, or leg of lamb. That's idiocy. Gewürztraminer is always going to have a role in the wine-drinker's menu and if it's not for me personally a big role, I'll still drink it, and for some editor behind a desk to suddenly decide it's going out of fashion is ridiculous. It's a pernicious influence on the wine market. It makes it faddish, like couture fashion, takes it out of the mainstream, makes it elitist, not an everyday activity."

Comparative tastings are good for the winemakers whose wines win. And one famous case was good for the American wine industry as a whole and, by extension (because it effectively ended the French illusion that they had a monopoly on quality), for the world wine industry. That was the comparison of twelve American wines with the very best of the French at a blind tasting in Paris organized by a British wine merchant and publicist. The Paris Tasting, as it became known, upset the wine world by demonstrating without possibility of error that the Americans were no longer producing large and clumsy wines that couldn't compare with the best of the Old World.

But tastings, and the celebration of winners, and the creation of celebrity winemakers, and the self-celebration of important writers, have their drawbacks. If one wine wins, others perforce lose, and the notion of individual taste loses currency. Tasting conditions have nothing to do with the conditions under which the wines will presumably be drunk, which is at table, with food. The matching of wine with food can yield up something better than either wine or food alone. Which in turn leads to other critical traps, in which a critic will insist that one wine goes best with fresh malpeque oysters and another one altogether with blue points. And don't *ever* have oysters Rockefeller unless you have yet a third kind of wine on hand.

Jensen is too savvy a winemaker, and his wines too consistent, to fall into the traps of faddishness. He has been the beneficiary of fashion as well as its critic, but this troubles him not at all. Consumers might come to his wines because they'd read about him in the glossy pages of *The Wine Spectator*, but he knew that once they'd come, they'd stay. And when late one evening I confessed that I was slowly abandoning my own unreasoning preference for cabernet sauvignon, he just grinned slowly, and said nothing. The bottle of Calera Jensen on the table said all that needed to be said.

XVI

*In which the wines are priced,
distributors are found, and the wines are
taken out into the world for their
final date with the consumer*

The final thing a winemaker can do for a wine is age it in the bottle at the winery for as long as possible—which means as long as he can afford—before putting it on the market. Calera's Central Coast pinot noir is usually sold soon after bottling. As a simpler wine, with fewer of the complicated chemical polymers, it doesn't improve as much with additional time in the bottle as the single-vineyard wines do.

Nor does it undergo the process that unnerves winemakers and still baffles the chemists, the phenomenon called "bottle shock" or "bottle sickness." Our '90 Jensen, like the great burgundies, on the other hand, is susceptible.

When they're bottled in the spring each year, the single-vineyard wines taste fresh, clean, delicious. "If you tasted the wine from the bottling tank you'd say, 'God, this is great.' Then, two months later, you open a bottle and you ask, 'What happened to this wine? Where did it go?' Because it tastes simple and one-dimensional ... flat and insipid." Bottle shock turns wines simple. They lose all their complexity, become one-dimensional, boring. I've never heard any chemist's explanation for this, but it happens to all good wines. Pinot noir, being the especially wine, tends especially to get bottle shock. About six months after being bottled they're at the nadir and then they start coming back, and once they've been in the bottle for about a year they're almost as good as they tasted when they were bottled, and perhaps starting to get better.

"It's a very scary process," Jensen acknowledges. "We certainly don't want our customers drinking the wines while they're in this state."

Our Jensen, perhaps bruised and indignant at being imprisoned in bottle, needs time to recover its dignity.

Fortunately, it will get it.

All nine hundred and seventy cases of the 1990 Jensen Mount Harlan pinot noir were stacked in the warehouse. But that didn't mean a customer could just walk in and buy a bottle, or a case, or a truckload. Nor did it mean that a restaurateur, hotelier or retailer could order whatever he wanted. Good marketing calls for a strategy that includes managing supply as well as shrewd pricing.

The first single-vineyard pinot noir vintage that Josh Jensen produced was tiny, a total of only one ton of grapes from twenty-four acres, or one twenty-fourth of a ton per acre, which yielded up just sixty cases of wine, almost small enough to put on the back of a pickup truck, which is how he delivered much of his wine in the early days. Or rather, a station wagon—you can't leave wine in the back of an open truck, not in Los Angeles; it won't be there after you come outdoors from your first sales call.

Leaving the winemaking to Steve Doerner, Jensen developed a small route, through San Bernardino down to Newport Beach, San Diego and back along the coast, through central Los Angeles. He'd deliver the zinfandels and samples of his single-vineyard pinot noirs, persuading chefs and sommeliers and retailers to taste on the spot: his corkscrew was his busiest sales tool. Later, when he started making chardonnay, he'd do the same with it.

He sold his wine to his friends, family, friends of family and family of friends. He used what connections he could. He'd twice met Ernest Gallo at a dinner at George Selleck's house. In 1984 Gallo expressed interest in Calera's zinfandels and asked if he could taste some of them. Jensen sent the legendary marketer, who along with his brother Julio had built up the world's largest winery, six different Calera wines and asked Gallo if he might perhaps recommend a few distributors. Although Calera's production was only a few bottles, Jensen had already won a few medals and thought Gallo might help. Surely the great man wouldn't feel jealous of a tiny winery? So he sent samples over to the Gallo winery. Several weeks went by and he heard nothing. He phoned, with no result. He phoned again. After several months of this, a short, terse letter arrived. "I see no future for any of your wines," Gallo wrote. "You should feel free to approach my distributors on your own, since I cannot recommend your wines to them."

Our bottle of Jensen carries a suggested retail price of thirty-five dollars a bottle. Settling on the price is a key decision for a winery; proper pricing can determine the success of its business. Josh does the final pricing at the last possible minute, but for the past few years the prices have shifted only slightly.

During 1992 the Central Coast chardonnay and pinot noirs (the vintages being sold were the '90s and '91s) retailed for fourteen dollars, a figure unchanged since the '86 vintage.

The first-ever offering of the single-vineyard wines were priced at eighteen dollars for the '78 vintage, which was sold entirely in half bottles in 1981, with a limit of three half bottles per customer. The eighteen-dollar price held for the first four vintages. The '82, which Jensen felt was his best wine to that time, went up a notch to twenty-three dollars for the Jensen and Reed and twenty-five for the Selleck. They stayed at that level for another three or four years, and then went up to thirty dollars for the Mills and the Reed, thirty-five for the Jensen and Selleck, where they've been ever since.

"When we came out with our first vintage of pinot noir, I set the price deliberately high, at eighteen dollars a bottle. In a way the price didn't matter, only the idea of the price level did. There'd been some word of mouth about the wines, which helped, and it was such a tiny quantity, really, that we could have priced it anywhere we wanted and it would have sold. It wasn't going to make a whole lot of difference to our cash flow. It almost didn't matter in terms of cash or profit. But eighteen dollars was higher than almost anybody was pricing American pinot noirs at that point, so it seemed like a good number to go in with, to stake a claim, to assert something about our product. People said to me, 'Why don't you price it at seven-fifty now and go up to eighteen dollars later?' but I didn't want to get customers used to paying seven-fifty, because they'd be ticked off when we raised the price to eighteen. We do get people saying our wines are too expensive, but at least they can't say, 'I used to buy it for seven-fifty and now it's thirty-five bucks and that's five times the price and that's a ripoff.'

"I never thought in my wildest dreams that our wines would be priced at thirty or thirty-five dollars, but I did think they'd get up to twenty-five or some such. So I didn't want to start low and travel all that distance."

How are prices set?

"It's quite subjective, a lot of it. I look at three things. First is the quality of the wine we're pricing relative to the competition, other American pinot noirs as well as burgundies. Secondly, I look at where we've been in pricing and how long we've been there. Thirdly I factor in where we want to be in terms of a long-term pricing strategy. In other words, do we eventually want to get our wine to be three hundred dollars a bottle? No, I don't think so. Do we eventually want to be forty dollars a bottle? Probably, but I'm not in a hurry."

Note that there's no consideration given here—none—to what the wine actually costs to produce. Calera sells almost all its wines through distributors for exactly half the suggested consumer retail price. But when Josh sets the price, whether thirty or thirty-five dollars a bottle, he still has no idea if that bottle cost him a dollar or sixteen dollars to make. He only finds out what his "cost of goods sold" and "gross margins" are from his accountant every spring. For years he had to sell the wines below the level of profitability. Now he makes money. But he can't base his wine pricing on what it costs to make the stuff. He prices it according to what will fly over the long haul "out there" in the martketplace.

"So ... we're pretty much a price leader for American pinot noir. There are a couple of wines at our level and there are a couple just above us. We'll watch this closely. I don't want to be too aggressive in getting out in front of the competition, and the fact is that we're making nice profits now. We can make money at this level."

Pricing, therefore, is based partly on availability (yield), partly on demand, partly on what the competition is charging for similar wines and partly on a long-term strategy. "You figure out what it costs you to grow it and make it and what it costs you to live, and that's what the wine should cost. You don't raise your prices just because you know you can get it. You don't want to alienate your customers, because your long-standing customers got you to where you are now."

The release or offering date, as the wines coming onto market is called, will differ each year depending on the yield and the nature of the wines—hard, closed wines should be kept in the winery longer, and Calera has sometimes released a younger vintage before an older one.

Each vineyard's wines are sold at different times, starting in the spring. As they sit in the warehouse, Josh formulates plans for release. For example, he could put the Reed out in February, the Jensen in May, the Mills in September and the Selleck the following

February. The timing would depend on the market. Four different releases a year would probably overstrain the market and would lessen the chances of each wine getting reviewed; on the other hand, releasing them all at once would get them reviewed, but only once — and they'd be compared to each other instead of to the competition.

These reviews are important. Especially for a new winery, but even for the established ones. Many retailers take the reviewers' judgments seriously and base their orders accordingly.

In the early years, this was particularly frustrating. "Every year we made a better pinot noir. One year the reviewers said we were better than everyone except X. The next year we'd be better than everyone except Y. Finally, we were judged the best pinot noir in California. Then Robert Parker lowered the boom and said that Oregon was where the best pinots were being made. Suddenly, being the best in California didn't seem to mean a damn thing. Then he lowered the boom on Oregon too, and since then we've been given generally positive reviews, especially by Parker but by others too."

In October 1992, Josh was still mulling the strategy for marketing the '90s. "One of the things spreading out the releases does is give us the option to deal with the bottle age of the wines. I'm pretty locked into the Reed in February and the Jensen in May. September I'm still mulling over. On the one hand, we had a terrific harvest in '92 and we've got a very large — for us — volume of '92 wines on the horizon. We have to plan for that. The year that we had the tiny crop — 1988 — we doubled up and sold two pinot noirs at each release because there was so damn little that I didn't want our customers to say, 'Oh well, it's not even worth thinking about.' So the Selleck and Mills were offered at the same time, and the Reed and the Jensen at the same time, one of the large vineyards with one of the small. At least the total number of boxes going to the customers would make some sense. That meant a whole year's worth was released in less than a year. With the '89s we staggered it again, by releasing the Reed last September, the Jensen in February, the Mills in May and the Selleck this September. We bought some time that way, and I want to do so again with the '90s and with the '91s. It will be three or four years from now before we release the '92s, so I'm not sure how we'll handle them. We'll keep ruminating until the right pattern emerges.

"I think the '90s will get to a stage of drinkability sooner than any vintage we've had since '86, maybe '84. The '84s were soft and silky for us, because our wines tend to be big and powerful and closed-in when young. The '84s and '86s were quite soft and accessible and elegant for Calera pinot noirs and the '90s have that character too. They won't be wines you'll have to keep for at least ten years, which is what the '88s are like. Nor will they be like the '85s and '87s, which you'll want to keep at least five years. Even though they're from a small-crop, one-ton-per-acre harvest, they'll be wines that will taste quite nice when relatively young. Young meaning when we release them, and the year after that."

In the first few years, while he was still selling his wine door to door in a station wagon, Josh developed his mail-order business. The first list consisted of everyone he knew, his family, and everyone his family knew. It has been amplified and purged many times since then, but his mail-order customers are still the first to get access to each vintage. Partly out of loyalty and partly because they are the most profitable sales for the winery.

He may be a man who markets on intuition, but he has developed a marketing system that is straight MBA and is designed to maximize sales across the production board.

Clients are divided into three categories.

The first is the mailing-list customer, individuals who order directly from the winery. They account for five percent of the volume and ten percent of the winery's revenue, almost all of that to California consumers or to visitors to the winery.

The second is the wholesaler. For the first ten years, Jensen spent most of his energy building a national reputation and a national distribution network. As a result, his wines are available in forty-four of the fifty American states. Calera now has wholesale distributors in most major U.S. markets, and those wholesalers account for eighty-five percent of Calera's revenues. About forty percent of the product is sold in

California. The other big markets are New York/New Jersey, Virginia, Washington D.C., Baltimore, Texas, Chicago and Florida.

The third category is the export market to twelve countries, primarily Britain, Canada, Japan, Germany, Australia, Belgium and the Netherlands; export business is now about ten percent of the total production. In addition, in those markets where the only "customer" is a large state bureaucracy, like Ontario, Calera has a commission agent in place.

The system he has set up is simple and much copied. Except for individual mail orders, all customers are required to buy a certain quantity of the workhorse wines, the Central Coast chardonnays and pinot noirs, before being allowed to purchase the single-vineyard pinot noirs, the Mount Harlan chardonnay or the viognier. Jensen puts it the other way around, arguing that customers are "rewarded" with the single-vineyard pinot noirs in the proportion that they buy the central coast wines. So if a large wholesaler buys two percent of the total production of the Central Coast wines one year, he gets two percent of the premium wines the next.

"We send out an offering letter to each distributor at each offering date, three times a year, in February, May and September. Based on their purchase of our mainstay Central Coast wines the year before, we offer them X cases of the premiums—say the '90 Jensen and the '91 Mount Harlan chardonnay. We reserve a small quantity for private direct consumer sales, but we sell the rest this way. Say we make a thousand cases of Jensen and we figure we're going to sell five percent to our mailing list, or have already sold five percent to our list, and five to ten percent to our export markets. That leaves eighty-five percent, or eight hundred and fifty cases, for our U.S. distributors. So, for example, a distributor who bought ten percent of Central Coast the year before would get ten percent of the Jensen, or eighty-five cases. He doesn't of course have to take the premium wines. In recent years it would almost be a relief if a distributor whom we offered thirty cases to said it's too expensive and declined. That would give us some extra cases to satisfy those who run out. But no one has been turning down the single vineyards."

Part of his problem is inventory control and that depends on yield. U.S. wholesalers are the core of his business and he needs to keep them happy. He needs to have enough Selleck and Jensen and Reed and Mills and viognier to offer them in amounts in which they don't feel they're getting short-changed. If he sold all the Jensen to his mailing list, the distributors would lose interest, even in good years. It would be profitable in the short term, but suicide in the long term, because it would alienate his distributor network.

Jensen is a strong proponent of exporting. He'd like his exports to grow to as much as twenty percent of sales by 1995. He wants his wines available as widely as possible, on the grounds that his reputation can only be enhanced by a presence in overseas markets. Also, it's a hedge: since 1986, wine consumption in the U.S. has gone down every year and as a sometimes prudent businessman, he doesn't want all his eggs in one national basket—America, after all, was a country that just a few decades ago outlawed wine altogether.

So his prices are lowest for his foreign buyers. Of course they have to pay more to get the wines there, plus tariffs, but the winery nets less.

Through the 1980s England accounted for eighty percent of Calera's exports. It wasn't hard to figure out why—a sophisticated clientele existed in a country that produces virtually no wine, so for at least a century England has been the freest of the world's wine markets. The French don't drink Italian wines and the Italians don't drink German wines, but the English are willing to consider wines from all countries.

In 1992, for the first time, Japan edged out England as Calera's biggest market.

Writing in his own wry style in one of his newsletters, Jensen described the export business:

"I find myself constantly explaining to our Danish importer that he can't order only Jensen pinot noir. Yes, I understand that everyone in Denmark is named Jensen, so that's what they all want. But we can't sell our wines that way. Switzerland for some reason wants only Selleck pinot noir. So we set up certain ratios in which we 'suggest' how they order our wines, and do our best to hold the line.

"Sometimes we get labeling, invoicing or documentation instructions from our importer that conflict with the instructions from his government. In the worst cases, both these sets of instructions will conflict not only with each other but also with orders issue by a sort of super government, the EC.

"Then what do you do? Our fearless office staff just forges ahead, letting no obstacle block their path to Export Heaven. But I'd be less than candid if I implied that they share my love of exporting. The paperwork is just mind-boggling. We now have about 5,000 different importer's strip labels in our arsenal, but we never seem to have the right one. And we are often asked to remove the U.S. government required health warning labels. Most other countries think these things are a real joke. What's more, for the EC we have to white out the words 'Contains sulfites,' so beloved of our own government. Those words are illegal in the EC.

"One way I'll try to motivate my staff so they'll complete the blizzard of paperwork is to read them lengthy quotes from overseas publications that write about Calera. Those written in English I can handle. French too. I also pretend I can translate all the others. German, Swedish, Italian, no problem. Estonian, Turkish, Bantu, Hungarian, Hindi, you name it, I'll give them the gist of the article. Often these translations include very specific and praiseworthy mention of the excellence of the Calera forms, shipping documents, paperwork and special labeling. Our happy staff is constantly amazed that wine writers in these far-off countries know the names of individual Calera employees and single them out for the accuracy, elegance and clarity of their work ..."

Sometimes, marketing has peculiar national hazards, and commenting on these can be occasionally ... counter-productive. Here's Josh on one of the state liquor boards, the Liquor Control Board of Ontario: "Sometimes your actual customer, when exporting, is a government. Good god! Canada is a capitalist, free market country, right? Well, it turns out that if you're going to export to Canada, the people on the other end doing the buying aren't really people at all, but government bureaucrats! We sell to the liquor authorities in three Canadian provinces, British Columbia, Alberta and Ontario. The

Liquor Control Board of Ontario is the worst. They try to place the craziest orders, and then typically take two or three months beyond the due date on the invoice to pay you. A few years ago they did a lab test on one of our wines, and decided something was wrong with the wine. They destroyed the entire ten case shipment (or said they did) without notifying us. We only learned about it six months later when we were making our 50th attempt to get them to pay. Needless to say, they never paid. What are you going to do, sue them? In their own courts? And why do we put up with this kind of tomfoolery? Because Toronto, the capital of the Province of Ontario, is the biggest city and the most important wine market in Canada. And Canada, as a country, is the largest export market for American wines."

Then, by the time he wrote his Summer 1992 mailer, he had discovered another important fact about the LCBO:

"ERRATA

"I'd like to correct a typographical error that somehow appeared in our last brochure, concerning the Liquor Control Board of Ontario, Canada (LCBO). I really don't know how such a thing could have occurred, probably due to my having gotten so 'care-worn' and 'weather-beaten' over the years, but apparently our brochure described a previous unhappy experience with the LCBO and may or may not have concluded with the words, 'The LCBO is the worst.'

"As luck would have it, shortly after we mailed out that brochure, our agent in Ontario, a solid, hard-working wine guy, got one of the biggest orders we've ever had, for 329 cases of wine, from the LCBO. That was when the comments allegedly contained in our brochure were brought to the attention of the highly respected Board members and the many fine, upstanding, diligent employees of the LCBO. They called our agent in on the carpet and, as we say out here in the west, worked him over pretty good. The alleged comments that may or may not have been printed in our mailer—almost certainly by typographical error, if in fact they were printed—damn near queered this giant order.

"If it was I who wrote the ill considered passage that may or may not actually have been printed in our brochure—and we (note the use of 'we' all of a sudden) are neither confirming nor denying that we ever wrote such a thing—it was not at all 'intellectual' on our part. If I wrote it, I was probably the victim of being too 'confident' of the accuracy of my own position on the matter.

"Be that as it may, I want to go on record as saying that in placing that one order the LCBO became ONE OF THE BEST, and when they paid us in full and on time the brilliant visionaries who make up the LCBO, and their many loyal, hard-working employees—and in fact all the beautiful, congenial and far-sighted residents of the entire Province of Ontario —immediately became THE BEST."

Calera sells a case of Central Coast wine direct to a consumer for a hundred and fifty one dollars and twenty cents—twelve bottles at fourteen, less ten percent full-case discount. That same case to U.S. distributors is eighty-four dollars. And that same case to export markets is seventy-five, nine dollars less. "It's a significant discount. And that's because I want to have our wines in Tokyo, Sydney, London, Toronto, Berlin. To keep their shipping costs reasonable, exporters consolidate orders from different wineries to make up a full container load, which can be six hundred or eleven hundred cases, ordering twenty cases from this winery, a hundred and twenty cases from that winery, sixty cases from this one.

"So inventory control is very important, and quite complicated, especially when you make three hundred and one cases of this and a hundred and ninety-two cases of that, and we have wine in half bottles and magnums as well as regular bottles."

Only the week before, he said, because of the order from the LCBO, they had been forced to count the boxes in their own storage and their shipper's warehouse, California Wine Transport (CWT) in San Jose, and discovered to their surprise that they were completely out of the '89 Selleck, except for the ten cases they kept back for the winery's "library" or archive of wines. "That, of course, affects our offerings. I sit down, usually in early January, and I project what I think we'll sell that year. For January '93 it was the '91 Central Coast chardonnay, the '91 Central Coast pinot noir, and I projected that we'd sell the entire production of the Chardonnay and the ten thousand cases of the pinot noir in 1993. We were also to be offering the '90 single-vineyard pinot noirs, so I took the total production of each of those and the '92 viognier and '91 Mount Harlan chardonnay, and I take ten percent of each and that's what I offer as a package to our importers overseas. They have to order in that ratio."

The following day I went to visit Jensen at his booth at the California Wine Experience, at San Francisco's Marriott Hotel. It cost me a hundred dollars just to get into the tastings. The hotel ballroom was jammed to the point of unpleasantness.

Jensen was pouring his Central Coast pinot noir and chatting to customers. I saw Ernest Gallo sniffing a glass at another table, Francis Ford Coppolla holding forth to a slightly awestruck crowd (wine people can be snobs, but they know a star when they see one; some of them had probably sat through his lecture earlier in the day: "Winemaking and filmmaking: a parallel experience"). Robert Mondavi was there. So was Joy Sterling and her father Barry. And winemakers and proprietors from a hundred and forty-five other premium wineries in the state.

The Grand Tastings, as they were described, took place in one of the ballrooms of the Marriott. For my hundred dollars I got a tasting book, with the labels and descriptions of all the participating wineries, and as many glasses for tasting as I needed. The wineries were in four aisles, and off to the right was a food area, cheeses, pâtés and terrines, bowls of fruit. For another couple of hundred I could have attended other lectures, a breakfast talk by Marvin Shanken, a lecture on wine and your health (a bow to Josh's eco-terrorists), a talk by Oz Clarke of the London *Daily Telegraph* on the new classic wines (by no coincidence at all the title of his new book—why else would he have flown in from Britain for a thirty-six-hour trip?).

I asked Josh later how important these shows were.

"Absolutely necessary to be there," was his response.

✿   ✿   ✿

Because about twenty percent of small California wineries operate on
the edge of bankruptcy, much depends on public acceptance and therefore public relations and promotion. As Lee Stewart, a legend in
California wine and owner of the former Souverain winery, once put it,
"Any jackass can make wine, but it takes a super jackass to market it."

Even the name, Calera, was chosen with a eye on the markets.

"I think we looked at about a thousand names before deciding on
Calera, which is the Spanish word for limekiln. It has a nice connection to our limestone theory, which is that limestone is critical for
good pinot noir. And it's a pretty-sounding word and easily pronounced in most languages."

Labels, too, are an important part of the image. Jensen asked Jim
Robertson, whose design and bookmaking firm in Covelo, California,
is called Yolla Bolly Press, to design his labels.

"For me, the classic wine label is Château Lafite-Rothschild,
which has only seven words on it." (This is not a label to run on endlessly about whether it goes better with fish or fowl, or to wax elo-
quent about the vinification techniques or the *terroir*.) "My winemaking is Burgundian, but as far as labeling is concerned I like the
style of that Lafite label. It simply says, 'Here I am, take it or leave
it.' So I tried to emulate that." In the Burgundian fashion, Jensen
wanted his labels to show the vineyard name bigger than the company name. "At first, Jim just couldn't fathom that. So I sent him
some (empty) bottles of burgundy, and then he saw how the name of
the vineyard parcel was always more prominent than the company
name, and then he got it."

So the early labels said:

> "CALERA
> JENSEN
> California Pinot Noir
> Table wine
> Produced & bottled
> by Calera Wine Company
> Hollister, California"

Little has changed since. The "California" has been dropped and the "Mt. Harlan" added, and Josh added the word "grown." So the labels now read:

"CALERA
JENSEN
Mt. Harlan Pinot Noir
1989
Grown, produced & bottled
by Calera Wine Company
Hollister, California
Table Wine"

This "Table Wine" business rankles some. Under U.S. government law, "table wine" is a legal term describing a wine containing between eleven and fourteen percent alcohol. Most wines fall into this category. Why is it important? Because this is also a tax category. Wineries pay excise taxes to both the federal and state governments based on which tax class they're in. Wines below eleven percent alcohol pay the least. Table wines pay what you might consider "normal" taxes, if such a thing is possible. These have risen steeply in recent years. Wines above fourteen percent, called "dessert wines" by the federal government (ports and sherries would be examples) pay much higher taxes. Sparkling wines pay the highest of all. All these taxes are paid at the producer level, by wineries, twice a month, on wines that are taken out of the bonded portion of their warehouse. The whole thing makes Jensen's teeth grind.

"The rest of the packaging is important too," Jensen said, as he poured a glass of pinot noir for a thirsty seeker after truth at the Marriott. "It's all part of the wine's image and positioning. The labels we've discussed. But even the bottles. I'm using imported French bottles for my premium wines. If you're going to charge thirty dollars a bottle for your product, it should be properly packaged, and the French bottles have an opulent look. I buy the best, the longest corks, with the winery name and the vintage date stamped on them. And, until recently, classic lead-foil capsules, maroon for the reds, yellow or cream for the whites."

He motioned to the capsule he'd just stripped from another bottle of Central Coast. "They've now banned lead in California, although they've been using it in Europe for centuries without hazard, but the policy czars here are convinced that it'll poison everyone." He has tried—and rejected—aluminum as a substitute ("Wait until you see how many sommeliers have cut fingers next year") and has adopted a heat-shrink plastic that is transparent, rather like a thick Saran wrap, with a small metal disk at the top to denote the wine's color.

I moved out into the crowded ballroom. The room was abuzz with conversation, punctuated by the peculiar gurgle-gargle and ringing spits of the wine world. Otherwise the atmosphere was the same as any other trade show, a mix of enforced jollity, anxiety, weariness and deal-making. I tasted a few pretty ordinary wines, but was suddenly thrilled with a 1990 Acacia pinot noir, from their St. Clair vineyard in Carneros, an extraordinary complex of fruit and oak that jolted me into remembering why I was there. Apart from being briefly sidetracked by a wonderful sangiovese 1990 from Atlas Peak Vineyards, which, though a small Napa winery, is owned by Bollinger of France, Antinori of Italy and a giant British brewery, and an exotic blend of grenache, syrah and mourvedre from Bonny Doon, I stayed with pinot noirs where I could find them. There weren't that many, ten from a hundred and forty-five wineries, but there were a few outstanding wines, among them Ken Brown's Byron pinot noir 1990 from Santa Barbara county (owned by the Mondavis but with Brown as winemaker); and Robert Stemmler's fine 1988, from Sonoma, one of the few wineries other than Calera to use native or natural yeasts for fermenting pinot noir. There were also a few that seemed to me thin and insipid, and I wondered why they had been brought to the show—did bottle shock take them by surprise? I went so far as to venture a tactfully phrased question to a young man at one of the offending wineries, but he just snarled and I moved off.

The heartbreak grape, clearly, was still breaking a few hearts, though it surprised me it was doing so quite so publicly.

❖   ❖   ❖

Once the wines leave the winery or the San Jose warehouse (once, that is, the excise folk have taken their cut), they seem to exist only in sealed trucks, in bonded premises or in computer memories. Where do they go?

I followed our bottle through a customer-consignment invoice on Calera's computer to the shipper in San Jose. From there it was packed into a massive semi-trailer with the products of a dozen other wineries; this trailer then headed cross-country for the east coast, a bootleg hijacker's wet dream. It crossed the desert in one pass, its refrigeration unit going full blast, passed over the prairies in a day and a half, and entered New Jersey no more than four days after it left. A few minutes after ten on a winter's morning it arrived in Somerville, New Jersey, the massive premises of Lauber Imports Ltd., where it became the property of burly, efficient men with forklifts, one pallet among thousands in a vast warehouse. The Calera label was nowhere to be seen, only an anonymous warehouse docket number. If it weren't that Mark Lauber and his father specialize in wine, and are as much wine lovers as wholesalers, it might as well have been sardines, or computer motherboards, or footstools, or dental equipment, or canned peas. But the number could also be found in the memory banks of Lauber's computer system, where it was clearly identified by its place and name of origin (Calera, Hollister, California) and by its eventual consignee, one Peter Morrell. I found that the bottle was destined to take one more journey, this time to mid-town Manhattan.

The Morrell and Co. store on Madison Avenue is where our original dinner table host had purchased our Jensen pinot noir for his dinner party.

Morrell and Co. is on the ground floor of a banal high rise between 54th and 55th. There's nothing banal about the interior, however. Peter Morrell, the big, bluff, outgoing chairman, wine buyer, bon vivant and chief bottlewasher, second-generation owner of a family business, has managed to impose a kind of measured calm on the store, with its wooden bins and attentive staff; and a much

more disheveled kind of order in the basement, where the stock-
rooms are, and in the sub-basement, where his cluttered office is to
be found. He also operates a warehouse on E. 33rd St., and another
temperature- and humidity-controlled warehouse for customers who
want to store their own collections in bonded and air-conditioned
safety. The store is a comforting place, with wooden bins of wine on
three walls. There was a collection of ports on display, a range of
sweet *eisweins*, a series of unusual California chardonnays, an excellent selection of burgundies and a sprinkling of odd lots and specials,
mostly French and California, but also Italian, Spanish, Aussie and
other wines, including a few from South Africa, like Nederburg and
Kanonkop. I looked to see if there were any from the old de Villiers
estate called Landskroon outside Paarl, but there weren't.

I reached Morrell's office by winding down a very tight spiral staircase to the stockroom level, then another staircase to the sub-
basement. His office is not the home of an anal-retentive person. Its
dominant mode is clutter. There were piles of paper everywhere,
boxes, crates, bags of bottles, some full and some half empty, standing, lying, jumbling up his desk. On the floor, a bottle of Chassagne-
Montrachet was standing upright on the carpet next to an anonymous
wine from the Midi. Just outside the door was a cardboard box of
odd lots, waiting to accumulate enough bottles to justify a tasting.
These are samples dropped off every day by hopeful winemakers,
wholesalers and agents—"missionarymen" for the wineries, in the old
phrase. There was also a crate of Pauillac, and on the wall certificates
of various honors, French and American, including one from le Grand
Conseil, l'académie du vin. Behind Morrell's desk (where a computer
was perched precariously on some sort of makeshift shelf) were tot-
tering piles of papers and looseleaf binders containing every imagin-
able wine publication, up-to-date and well-thumbed.

Morrell is a fan of Calera's wines. "It's important to us. We sell a lot
of it. I've been following Josh for ten years, and every year at the vintage change we open a bottle of the current vintage and a bottle of the
new one, and up to now we have had no cause to worry. There are no
surprises. There's just the familiar derivative, consistent quality. I

always seem to prefer last year's to the current one, which I think is a good sign." He likes Calera because it is fairly priced and has the complexity of style that he personally likes. "We sell out quickly. In retrospect, I should have held back six bottles of each Calera so we could keep some." In 1992, Morrell and Co. sold thirty-one hundred bottles of Central Coast chardonnay through their warehouse, and a thousand and fifty from the store, for a total of three hundred and forty-six cases. "Not bad for one store, eh?"

He sells only small quantities of the single-vineyard pinot noirs. "The consumer here is pinot ignorant. They don't know anything about pinot noir, which is a pity because it's a lovely grape." He has five cases left of the Central Coast pinot noir, having ordered twenty-four cases altogether.

Of the Jensen, only a case or two were ordered. Only two bottles were left.

I pointed to the wine periodicals and asked him how he made his selections from the vast inventory of wines available to him.

"You can't possibly taste all the wines there are," I said.

"Yes we do," he said, misunderstanding. "At least ninety percent of the stock we taste personally. "

"No," I said, "I mean, of all the wines in the world, how do you choose what to stock?"

Retailers, he said, find their wines through personal contacts, history, gossip, tours of the wine-producing regions, by dinners and formal tastings, and by attending wine shows. Bottles come from sales people, missionarymen and anyone who drops by with a suggestion. Other ideas come from a voracious reading of the wine press. A good review will prompt an order, or at least a request for a sample, almost immediately, which is why the critics have such power in the industry. "These are generally experienced people and we learn to trust certain of them. They are reliable guiding lights. They miss a few, but not many." He also visits as many wineries as he can. "There's no substitute for experience; I want to check the dedication and techniques of the winemaker, to see if he is serious about what he does. Was the wine I tasted a fluke? Will he last? Wine after all is fifty percent nature and fifty percent man. That human fifty percent can make all the difference between great wine and mediocre wine."

While we were talking there was a steady stream of calls. The Tastevin Society wanted to borrow a couple of barrels for their annual dinner, as they do every year; a caller wanted him to represent Georgian wines from Russia and Ukraine (he declined, averring that he is not an importer); people wanting to buy, to sell, or just to invite him to dinner, lunch, a drink ... Colleagues called, and customers.

Between calls, he punched up Calera on his computer, using sophisticated inventory-control software that he devised himself. It allows him to search for and tabulate by customer, by winery, by wine, by order, by quantity or by date. He hit a few buttons and a list of Calera's customers started to scroll up the screen. It was a formidable list, taking several minutes to roll by. I noticed a few who had ordered Calera by the case lot. They were individual collectors who bought in thousand-dollar lots.

He punched up the smaller number of clients who had bought the Calera single-vineyard wines. The Sellecks scrolled by, and the Reeds. There were the Jensens, the 1990s, the 1989s, the '88s, the '87s ... I saw a familiar name, and an address in Mount Vernon.

I had found the bottle that started it all.

When our host pulled the cork on his bottle of Calera Jensen '87, he was doing something Americans don't do very often. Or at least, far fewer times than Europeans.

At the beginning of the 1970s, Americans drank only six bottles of wine a year each, a little more than a gallon. Ten years later, as they turned away from hard liquor, they were drinking more—the national consumption had gone up to four hundred and fifty million gallons by the beginning of the 1980s, an increase that exceeded the increase in the adult population, but not by much.

In the 1970s red wine was drunk at most American tables where wine was drunk at all. As California's propaganda industry moved into a higher gear and consumption started to go up, white wine soon began to predominate, partly because newly converted wine drinkers favored whites, easier on palates accustomed to pop and beer, and partly because the industry wanted it that way. Josh Jensen had said of his viognier that it was "the perfect accountant's wine—it demands to be bottled early and sold early" and that was true of all white wines relative to red. They could be released for sale sooner and therefore bring in cash earlier. By 1981, three bottles of white wine were sold for every bottle of red.

By the mid-1980s, wine was becoming something of a status symbol. The spritzer replaced the martini as the beverage of choice for lunch. The idea that wine was something more than a beverage seeped into public consciousness. The wine press on the one hand pushed the idea that drinking wine was pure pleasure, and on the other that fine wine, and esoteric knowledge about fine wine, was something of a social determinant, a denoter of status. This tiresome notion was reinforced by the arcane and snobbish rituals of the industry itself and the parvenu one-upmanship of the newly converted moneyed classes. For a while wine became even more divorced from its agrarian roots; wine drinking became associated with wealth and privilege on the one hand, and artistry on the other.

Then, in the late 1980s, as the faddishness of some wine drinking faded and as the health lobbyists joined in an unholy alliance with the puritan killjoys, wine consumption started to fade again.

It's something that worries the industry. Peter Morrell's father barely kept his business alive the last time such an alliance happened, during Prohibition, by selling a little wine "for medicinal or religious uses only."

Morrell is still angry about this and referred to the rules governing his industry as "prehensile," which I interpreted to mean something ridiculously archaic rather than grasping, but which on reflection he probably meant literally. After Prohibition was repealed, which took an amendment to the U.S. Constitution, the control of alcohol was left to the individual states and so there are more than fifty sets of rules concerning the sale of "beverage alcohol," a catchall definition that includes beer, wine and spirits. Even in New York, among the most enlightened of the states, Morrell is not allowed to sell beer, or even a corkscrew, in his store, only wine and liquors. Grocery stores, on the other hand, can sell beer but not wine.

Fumbling through a stack of papers, Morrell pulled out a clipping from the *New York Times*, and pushed it across the table. "Read it and weep for America," he said. The clipping concerned a young couple in the town of Brevard, North Carolina, who operate a restaurant, or at least did until they applied for and got a wine license. Transylvania County, North Carolina, was at that point dry, although it did have one state-run liquor store and allowed wine, but not beer, to be served by permit in restaurants. The restaurant went bankrupt because the townsfolk boycotted the place for serving wine with meals.

Other states are even worse. Pennsylvania, like Ontario, has a state liquor authority that hedges the sale of wine with dozens of idiotic regulations. The federal government has insisted on a health warning on every bottle, and legislation has been proposed that would make it obligatory for each label to show a pictograph of a pregnant woman and a giant wineglass with a red slash through it. A California politician proposed a special tax on wine to provide funding for fighting crime. There are even moves to have no-drinking sections in California restaurants, following the egregious example of the nico-Nazis and their anti-smoking campaign. (To counter this trend somewhat, in October 1992 California's Beringer Vineyards won approval to hang a tag around the neck of one of their wines alluding to the possible health benefits of red wine. As evidence for their side, they quoted not only the French study that had discovered the stress-reducing ability of a moderate amount of wine, but also put forward a couple of eminent testimonialists, Thomas Jefferson and Jesus Christ.)

Many in the wine industry watch all this with gloom and increasing alarm. Josh Jensen, for one, favors getting the government completely out of the wine business. "We are an industry that is highly regulated by a bunch of meddlesome bureaucrats who'd be better off breaking rocks somewhere than breaking the chops of peace-loving winemakers." He's not the only one who would like to keep wine out of the hands of pressure groups, politicians, hysterical moralists and kill-joys. The more rules and regulations there are, the less chance there'll be of making (or finding) idiosyncratic, personal, handmade, natural wines like Calera's own; the advantage will belong to the factory operation. Bureaucracy begets boring wine.

I remember a paragraph from Kermit Lynch, who was describing a pleasant afternoon after buying a quantity of light beaujolais. "No, we didn't discuss the pH, the oak, the body, the finish. But there was a gaiety to it, the tart fruit perfumed the palate and the brain ... Wine is, above all, pleasure. Those who would make it ponderous make it dull."

I thought back to our dinner in Mount Vernon. Josh Jensen's wine hadn't made the conversation more brilliant or the dinner guests more philosophical. The wine was barely noticed, except as a pleasant part of a pleasant occasion. Which is enough to ask of any beverage.

At the end of the evening, as the dishes were being done and the kitchen tidied, our host soaked the label off the bottle as an *aide mémoire*—he has a folder full of labels, each representing a pleasant memory. I looked at this folder some months later and found the Jensen label in a plastic sleeve, between an Inniskillin icewine from the Niagara Peninsula and an estate riesling from the south island of New Zealand. A few weeks after our visit, I noticed, our host had bought another Calera wine, the Central Coast pinot noir, and then a Calera chardonnay. Well, in one way they were just more bytes for the Calera databank, more dollars for the bottom line. But I knew Jensen would be pleased far beyond these mundane matters. By happenstance or shrewd marketing, he had captured another wine lover, yes. But because of his obsession with quality he had also become a page in a rich library of memories of a family he didn't know, while our host had in turn become part of the web of contacts that began in the gritty limestone soil of the Gavilan Mountains of central California. Not bad for the heartbreak grape.